The Bundesbank

Germany's Central Bank in the International Monetary System

Ellen Kennedy

CHATHAM HOUSE PAPERS

An International Economics Programme Publication
Programme Director: J. M. C. Rollo

The Royal Institute of International Affairs, at Chatham House in London, has provided an impartial forum for discussion and debate on current international issues for some 70 years. Its resident research fellows, specialized information resources, and range of publications, conferences, and meetings span the fields of international politics, economics, and security. The Institute is independent of government.

Chatham House Papers are short monographs on current policy problems which have been commissioned by the RIIA. In preparing the papers, authors are advised by a study group of experts convened by the RIIA, and publication of a paper indicates that the Institute regards it as an authoritative contribution to the public debate. The Institute does not, however, hold opinions of its own; the views expressed in this publication are the responsibility of the author.

CHATHAM HOUSE PAPERS

The Bundesbank

Germany's Central Bank in the International Monetary System

Ellen Kennedy

The Royal Institute of International Affairs

Pinter Publishers
London

© Royal Institute of International Affairs, 1991

RIIA Charity Reg. No. 208 223

First published in Great Britain in 1991 by
Pinter Publishers Limited
25 Floral Street, London WC2E 9DS

British Library Cataloguing in Publication Data

A CIP catalogue record for this book is available from the British Library

ISBN 0-86187-887-6 (Paperback)
     0-86187-151-0 (Hardback)

Reproduced from copy supplied by
Stephen Austin and Sons Ltd
Printed and bound in Great Britain by
Biddles Ltd

CONTENTS

PREFACE

This study of Germany's central bank began in 1988 and was completed during autumn 1990 – in a period, therefore, of dramatic political change. While it was being written, political revolution toppled the communist German Democratic Republic, making way for unification of the eastern Länder with the Federal Republic of Germany. West Germany's economic success played a major role in that transformation: as one poster in the Leipzig demonstrations after November 1989 demanded, 'Either the Deutschmark comes to us, or we'll go to the Deutschmark'. Having created one of the world's most stable and powerful currencies, the Bundesbank now has the task of 'protecting the currency' for a united Germany. In that task, past experience will shape its goals and monetary policies.

My thanks to the Directors and staff of the Deutsche Bundesbank for their assistance in carrying out this study, especially to Herr Manfred Körber. I am grateful to Dr Bernhard Blohm (*Die Zeit*), Dr DeAnne Julius (Chief Economist, Shell International), Dr Dieter Lindenlaub (Deutsche Bundesbank), Jim Rollo (International Economics Programme Director at the Royal Institute of International Affairs) and to members of the Chatham House Study Group for reading and commenting on an earlier version of the manuscript. To all my partners in conversation on the Bundesbank and its politics, a word of thanks. The errors which remain are mine alone.

This study was carried out under the auspices of the Royal Institute of International Affairs, and the customary 'Chatham House rules' apply to many of my sources.

November 1990   Ellen Kennedy

1
INTRODUCTION

This is a book about the Deutsche Bundesbank, the central bank of the Federal Republic of Germany, as a political institution.

From a country in ruins at the end of the Second World War, West Germany grew into one of the world's most powerful economies. A leading world exporter, the Federal Republic sits with Japan and the United States among the informal 'Group of Three' (G-3) industrial nations, which have more *de facto* power over the international economy today than the larger and more formal 'Group of Seven' (G-7).* Before the economic, monetary and social union of the two Germanies on July 1 1990, the Deutschmark had become an international reserve currency. As a united Germany emerges, the Bundesbank will control vital aspects of its development. Within the European Community (EC), soon to be the world's largest internal market, the Bundesbank can sometimes exercise decisive power over items on the economic and political agenda. Having created a stability bloc of low-inflation countries in Europe through its influence within the European Monetary System (EMS), Bundesbank policies can directly affect the domestic economic policies of Germany's EC partners. By any standard, then, the Bundesbank belongs to the small elite of national institutions that, for the foreseeable future, will influence the course of international politics.

And yet, despite Germany's key importance in the world economy, the political culture and institutions of the Federal

* The G-3 plus the UK, France, Canada and Italy.

1

Republic remain largely unfamiliar to outsiders. Chapter 2 locates the Bundesbank in the context of other German domestic institutions. Outside Germany the Bundesbank often appears as a monolithic structure unwavering in the fight against inflation, and excessively influencing the economies of other EC countries. Although that is little more than a caricature, the institutional characteristics of the Bundesbank make it very different from other central banks in Europe. The Bank of England and the Banque de France must follow the monetary and economic direction of government. The Bundesbank does not. The central banks of England and France are highly centralized. The Bundesbank is a federal institution. No other central bank in Europe and not even the United States Federal Reserve, on which the Bundesbank was modelled, enjoys the same degree of authority over monetary policy.

The reasons for the Bundesbank's unique character must be sought in the German state tradition and the practical lessons of recent German history. The decay of the Weimar Republic into dictatorship taught the founders of the second German republic powerful lessons about the dangers of violating the normative structure of the rule of law. A firm grasp of how legal norms and principles shape German politics is necessary if easy, but misleading, assumptions about why the Bundesbank does what it does are to be avoided.

Like the United States, Germany has a modern tradition of federal government going back to the foundation of the German Empire in 1871. Its attachment to federal structures is one expression of a shared commitment in the West to government under law and to the practical organization of checks and balances in a modern democracy. The Bundesbank is no exception to the overall pattern of public institutions in the Federal Republic. In a world where public policy is increasingly affecting economic policy, it is hardly surprising that commitment to constitutional government should extend to the monetary as well as the political sovereign. So, as a federal institution, the Bundesbank's organization and powers reflect the norms of the rule of law, or *Rechtsstaat*, in today's Germany and its institutional practice centres on a basic norm: protecting the currency against inflation. The Bundesbank example proves the general rule that in Germany the political axis is always only one dimension of public debate. The Bundesbank is an institution whose ethos cannot be fully understood merely as a technique or policy style. Rather, the cultural roots of an independent central bank run deep within the ideal of the *Rechtsstaat*.

In Chapter 3, the emphasis shifts to the way in which institutional responsibilities and their practice define the political field of the Bundesbank's activities. Endowed with so much legal autonomy in the discharge of its monetary functions that it is sometimes referred to as 'a fourth branch of government', the Bundesbank must still take account of the general economic policy goals set by Germany's political leadership.[1] The division of powers in Germany's economic constitution between the federal government and the Bundesbank has been a constant reference point in political debate since the enactment of the Bundesbank Law in 1957. At home the Bank faces no serious challenge to its authority, but the growing importance of largely uncontrollable international factors, arising directly from Germany's prominence in the international economy and its leading role in the European Community, affects the successful pursuit of its objectives.

Those larger circles of influence are the subject of Chapters 4 and 5. Chapter 4 traces the link between the Bundesbank's domestic policies and Germany's position in the international economy. The central theme here is the Bank's definition of 'imported inflation' as a phenomenon that plagues the Federal Republic more than the other major nations, and its efforts to limit the vulnerability of the domestic economy to external economic pressures. Not big enough to insulate itself from international economic pressures by retreating to the domestic market (as the United States can), the Federal Republic is too big to allow other nations to ignore movements in its economy.

In the wider international sphere the Bundesbank norm constitutes a significant limitation on Germany's political flexibility, and Chapters 4 and 5 indicate how normative considerations originating in the domestic German system impinge on the options of its political allies and trading partners as well. But as Germany's importance in the global economy and in Europe increases, the Bundesbank's situation is also changing. Its behaviour during the 1980s reveals a national institution struggling to manage sometimes anarchic international pressures without sacrificing its own institutional identity.

That is especially true in the context of European politics, where the Deutschmark's role as 'anchor currency' in the EMS and the size of its economy give Germany the leading role. As Chapter 5 shows, a succession of German governments have discovered that the Bundesbank norm can limit their room for manoeuvre on bilateral and multilateral issues. While policy-makers in the Bank tend to see their European obligations as another source of tension that might eventually reduce the efficacy of the Bundesbank norm, the story of the Bundesbank's management of the EMS is one of political skill in selling its standard of monetary management and the targeted use of economic power when necessary.

Finally, this study elaborates two general themes. First, a national political institution defined largely in terms of its domestic values and historical traditions now finds itself at the centre of international pressures at both regional and global levels. Its normative foundation as 'protector of the currency' often gives the Bundesbank its justification for the policies it pursues, sometimes in conflict with its major partners.[2] Second, in many respects the Bundesbank incorporates the ideals of an earlier age of political development. Largely immune to the pressures of pluralist politics, it sees itself as the representative of a good higher than particular interests, and that vision animates its policy attitudes. But are such principles justified in a democracy? The Bank is no longer a purely national institution. How will the normative power of law fare in the wider sphere of interests in which Germany's economic power now involves the Bundesbank? Both these questions – government by experts and the role of norms in political life – arise with particular force in German political culture. The reader interested in tracing them out in contemporary political practice could find no better object of study than the Bundesbank.

2
THE BUNDESBANK: ETHOS, ORGANIZATION, POWERS

From the 13th floor, directors of Germany's central bank can look out over the financial centre of Frankfurt. The towers of the Deutsche Bank, Commerzbank and Dresdener glisten in the middle distance, surrounded by the web of motorways that encircle the city. Every few minutes jets taking off and landing at Frankfurt International Airport cut through the skyline. A major world financial centre, Frankfurt has begun to rival New York, London and Tokyo.

This is contemporary Germany. A far cry from the devastation left behind in 1945, the Federal Republic today is a prosperous country whose exporting success – roughly one-third of its GDP – puts it within the most powerful economic circle in the world, the G-3. Yet the Germans were reluctant actors on this scene, only hesitantly taking over Europe's economic leadership and unwilling to translate economic clout into political muscle. Political revolution in the German Democratic Republic during the autumn of 1989 changed the international field of action for both Germanies. Less than a year later unification, for forty years almost universally regarded as an impractical constitutional goal, became a reality.

The existence of two capitals – political in Bonn, financial in Frankfurt – emphasizes the unique relationship between governmental power and monetary sovereignty in present-day Germany. Whatever the policy-makers in Bonn decide, the Bundesbank takes its own look and makes its own decisions about the country's monetary course. For the most part, both sides seem to like it that way, even if politicians downstream on the Rhein in Bonn have sometimes had reason to wish their central bank were less independent than it is.

The Bundesbank ethos

No public institution in Germany is free of the past and the Bundesbank is no exception. The Federal Republic has now outlived any of its constitutional predecessors on German soil since 1871 and produced a standard of living and a degree of political stability unmatched in modern German history, yet there are several crucial historical factors that have affected the operation and principles of the Bundesbank.

(a) Fear of inflation

Although it was not set up until 1957, eight years after the establishment of the Federal Republic, the Bundesbank inherited the monetary traditions of its predecessor, the Bank deutscher Länder (BdL), itself a product of the Allied occupation. Regulated by the Allied Bizonal Commission, the BdL carried out the currency reform of 1948, which West Germans remember as a kind of miracle. The value of the old currency (Reichsmark) had already been severely eroded by the National Socialists during the Second World War. Towards the end of the war money became virtually worthless; and with Germany's total defeat and division, the country sank into a black-market and barter economy. Nothing was available in the shops, and even the basics of food could be purchased only with foreign currency or by exchanging goods.

In the currency reform of 1948, the old mark was replaced by the present German currency, the Deutschmark (DM). On 20 June 1948 every person was allowed to exchange forty old marks for the same number of new ones. A further exchange in August 1948 allowed 20 new marks for the same number of old marks. The rate of 1:10 (one new mark for every ten old marks) applied to any amounts above that which were held by private persons in bank accounts. A further reform in October meant that people actually received about 65 new pfennigs for every one of their old marks. The effect on capital in the Western sector was dramatic. Private savings accounts were reduced from 68,963 billion old marks to 3,607 billion new marks, and capital held by firms and private persons dropped from 119,643 billion old marks to 9,205 billion new marks.[1] There was an immediate effect on supplies: the reforms were introduced on a

Sunday, and consumers found the shop windows full of goods on Monday morning. More importantly, the currency reform of 1948 provided the basis for a stable economic environment.

Germans in 1948 could still remember the dramatic effect of inflation after the First World War. In 1914 the dollar had been worth 4.2 marks, and half that in 1919. The mark steadily declined throughout the first years of the Weimar Republic until at the peak of inflation – in mid-November 1923 – a dollar was worth more than 4 billion marks. In the early 1920s paper money lost value by the hour, and men and women rushed to exchange it for whatever it would buy.

For millions of Germans [Gordon Craig has written] these figures created a lunatic world in which all the familiar landmarks assumed crazy new forms and all the old signposts became meaningless, in which the simplest of objects were invested by alchemy with monstrous value – the humble kohlrabi shamefacedly wearing a price-tag of 50 millions, the penny postage stamp costing as much as a Dahlem villa in 1890 – but in which all value was illusion and monetary fortune was fleeting.[2]

Trust in the country's currency was finally achieved by the *Rentenmark* reform of mid-November 1923. A body independent of government guaranteed a new basis for the currency and stopped the ocean of paper money which had engulfed Germany. This reform laid the foundations for five years of relative economic stability until the Republic, like all other industrialized nations, went into depression in 1929.

The social and political consequences of the great inflation of 1923 were profound. It wiped out personal savings and drastically transformed the representative value of money. Most people had to start all over again; solidly middle-class families found themselves in penury, and those who had loaned money in pre-inflationary marks lost virtually all of the value of their capital. Economic disaster was not really the worst of inflation's consequences. It undermined public confidence in governmental institutions and encouraged the growth of radical nationalist movements and communism. It counts as one of the certain causes of the ultimate political failure of the first Republic.[3]

7

The contrast between the Federal Republic's monetary stability after 1948 and the corresponding period of the Weimar Republic could not have been greater. After the First World War, Allied reparation demands contributed to Germany's financial chaos and kept political hatreds alive in Europe. Largely as a result of US policy, there was no repetition of that after the Second World War. Economic recovery in the Western zones of Germany and the success of the new currency were greatly aided by Marshall Plan capital approved by the US Congress in March 1948. Germany was also fortunate in having Ludwig Erhard as Economics Minister. Given a free hand to manage the return to civil production, Erhard put liberal economic principles at the foundation of a social market economy for the new Federal Republic.[4] Erhard's leadership galvanized the sheer determination of young Germans who had survived war and Nazi destruction to rebuild their country. Eager to live normal lives again after twelve years of dictatorship and war, this generation of Germans wanted to forget their past and get on with clearing away the physical rubble of their divided nation. Practical and hard-working, they had little time for politics and less time for ideals.

The unquantifiables of personalities and leadership in the founding generation of the Federal Republic were a crucial element in Germany's political and economic recovery. Enormous demand existed in the home market, and the biggest boost from outside came from production geared to the Korean War. Between 1950 and 1952 Germany had a real growth rate of 8.7%, with interest rates at a historic high level of 6% during 1951–2.[5] The BdL's success in managing Germany's money during periods of high growth remains a standard for the present-day Bundesbank.

The distinctive element in the Bundesbank ethos is a refusal to compromise on inflation. 'There is no such thing as a little bit of inflation', Bundesbank officials like to say; and the Bundesbank view has been constant on this issue. Even single-digit inflation destroys a currency's value over the medium term and gradually destroys the economy as a whole. Bundesbank Vice-President Helmut Schlesinger stresses this on practically every occasion; even while Germany was showing an increase of only 2.2% in consumer prices (in 1985), followed by zero inflation (during 1986), he continued to warn against inflationary pressures. Schlesinger's remark that 'the Bundesbank [has taken] steps to help the economy when it could do so without endangering the value of money' summarizes the Bank's attitude: i.e., the specific role of a central bank in a modern economy is identified as maintaining the stability of money, and it will support the government's general economic policy only so long as this goal is not jeopardized. A stable currency is 'the precondition of a functioning market economy and economic growth'.[6]

But the Bundesbank's working definition of inflation differs from this rhetoric, allowing for an 'unavoidable' rate of inflation determined by reference to expected growth in real output and prices. Its concept of 'inflation' therefore acts as a *normative* criterion for the development of Germany's domestic economy. Although its norm of stable currency remains constant, the Bundesbank definition of inflation in terms of tolerable deviations varies with its money supply targets. Differences of opinion between members of the Central Bank Council, particularly between Vice-President Schlesinger and the Bank's President, Karl Otto Pöhl, over inflationary dangers in specific circumstances are matters of emphasis, not signs of a break in the ranks of top management on the anti-inflation ethos. Pöhl takes obvious institutional pride in the Bundesbank's success in combating inflation, and uses it skilfully to bolster his own political position. A statement to commemorate the 40th anniversary of the 1948 currency reform stressed the Bank's extraordinary achievements in this respect: 'Forty years of economic success with an average inflation rate of 2.7%'.[7]

To the outsider the Bundesbank's fear of inflation looks unwarranted in the face of such figures. Much of the international pressure the Bank experienced from the early 1980s onwards expresses foreign impatience with its interpretation of the dangers of inflation. But these fears have to some extent been shared by the population at large. It is historical experience that determines a population's sensitivity in such matters. Responses to an English opinion poll in 1967, for example, showed that only 5% of those questioned had any idea of 'what inflation actually is', whereas a German poll the following year turned up 'crass differences at the information level' between Britons and Germans. The most significant finding was that Germans were much more prepared to give up wage increases if prices remained stable.[8]

The slogan 'protection of the currency' works in the monetary rhetoric of Bundesbank officials largely because of the devastating effects that two runaway inflations had on Germany's political and

9

social history in this century. The generation that experienced the social and political effects of hyperinflation in 1923 is gradually disappearing, however, and political leadership is passing to the postwar generation. There are some indications, too, that the West German 'inflation consensus' is less solid than it once was. For the German baby-boomers, unemployment is a greater fear than inflation. Almost twenty years after the 1968 survey, the Allensbach Institute again asked West Germans what they thought about the dangers of inflation. At a time when price increases were at a 30-year low, only 40% of those asked attributed this stability to success in fighting inflation; the rest could see no changes or had no opinion. Such results indicate that the 'psychology of money' is changing among West Germany's population, and the *Frankfurter Allgemeine* newspaper was quick to point out the consequences for the Bundesbank. If fear of unemployment became greater than fear of inflation, as it well may do after the influx of East German workers, the Bundesbank's traditional approach to monetary management would come under increased criticism from those who thought that 'monetary policy must at last be directed towards the goal of full employment'.[9]

(*b*) *German political culture*
Such changes in popular opinion have not affected the Bundesbank ethos and are unlikely to do so. While the practical questions of how best to manage Germany's monetary system become increasingly complex, forcing an international leadership role on the Federal Republic which it often seems to wish on others, its basic approach to such questions remains embedded in respect for the rule of law, and in the traditions of the professional civil service in Germany.

No institution in the Federal Republic can be understood without recognizing the influence of a firmly established *Rechtsstaat* culture on politics. The idea of the state as a legal system embodied in the concept of the *Rechtsstaat* appears very much like the Anglo-American notion of the 'rule of law', but the German tradition of political thought bestows an ideal dignity on the instruments of the state. These are not just the handy tools for practical politics that they seem to be for Americans and Britons, but instruments that express and create a public good beyond the interests of the market-place.

Bundesbank policy aims at a practical result ('stable money'), of course, but its normative character points beyond that towards a collective choice in German society, and an important element of political identity in the Federal Republic. Although it is not a constitutional branch like the judiciary, legislative or executive, the Bundesbank operates in a constitutive manner and its norm of monetary stability is more like a constitutional principle, such as private property rights, than like a simple directive or order, such as the price of postage. It acts in a legal context like the normative order of a constitution whose rules present a snapshot of the dimensions of reality at a particular time. Success depends on getting the focus clear enough but not so clear that it prevents us from seeing other pictures in the same frame. The Bundesbank Law belongs to a picture of the federal German constitution taken in the postwar years of recovery and restoration. Its fundamental norm embodies the values of a particular generation and its history. The meaning of those values, their acceptance and their political implications change over time, and much political struggle is focused on establishing an authoritative interpretation of these values.

In the area of monetary policy the Bundesbank guides the German economy by reference to its stability norm in much the same way that a constitutional court acts to interpret a state's basic rules. Its decisions, like the decisions of a court, are constitutive of the meaning of principles and norms that appear clear in theory but are open to variation in practice. Again, like a court deciding a case, the Bundesbank must make policy between two sets of concerns: its legal (or normative) obligations in public law, and the demands of the case before it. What 'protecting the currency' will mean in fact, then, depends on the Bank's judgment of complex and shifting particulars.

The civil service tradition in Germany plays a second and equally important role in the Bundesbank. Originating in the ideal of a non-political expert whose first duty is to serve the state, the civil service was idealized by the philosopher Hegel as the 'universal class' that did not represent any particular interest in society but stood for the ethical interest of the whole. Dedicated to professional objectivity in its treatment of public issues, the Prussian civil service of the end of the last century provided the model for Max Weber's concept of bureaucratic rationality. After 1945, discredited but still essential for rebuilding a new German state, the professional civil service was quickly enlisted by the Allied Military Governments to help run the country, but its status remained ambiguous until the Federal Constitutional Court ruled that there had been a break with history (*Traditionsbruch*) in May 1945. The Court's judgment put civil servants on a formally new legal footing in the Federal Republic, one which implied that 'public officials did not serve the state as a living and permanent continuity but the constitutional order' that existed at the time.[10]

Creation of a central bank

At its promulgation in 1949, the German Basic Law (*Grundgesetz*) foresaw the creation of a central bank but left specific provisions to later legislation. In fact Germany's central bank preceded its constitution by more than a year. The Allies' goal for German banking paralleled their aims for the country as a whole: to create decentralized, federal structures in a deliberate break with the unitary state tradition in Germany. The precursor of today's Bundesbank was a creation of the Allied Military Governments. In each of the German Länder (states), the American, British and French authorities set up *Landeszentralbanken* (Länder central banks) in their zones of occupied Germany, territory that became the Federal Republic in 1949. In addition, at British insistence, a central bank, called the Bank deutscher Länder (BdL), was established to act as a coordinating body for the Länder central banks. Its structure and powers closely resembled those of the present Bundesbank, with one important difference. Through an Allied Banking Commission, the occupying powers retained veto power over the policies of the BdL.[11] That power was never used, thanks largely to the political skill of the BdL's first president, Wilhelm Vocke, in coordinating the Bank's policy with that of the Allied Banking Commission. In 1950, after the Federal Republic had come into existence, the government drafted legislation whereby the BdL was provisionally established as West Germany's central bank and would no longer need to refer to the Allied Banking Commission.

In its first draft of the legislation, the government proposed a relatively decentralized institution and a federal committee on economic and monetary matters with strong governmental representation. In further draft legislation, in March 1951, the Economics Ministry under Ludwig Erhard suggested that the authority of the

12

Allied Banking Commission over the German banking system should be transferred to the federal government. The Central Bank Council of the BdL strongly objected, and much of the debate over the next six years centred on the issue of whether the nation's central bank should have independence from governmental control.[12]

When the Bank deutscher Länder was replaced by the Deutsche Bundesbank in 1957, it was the product of political compromise. Although the bankers carried the day, the Bundesbank Law of 1957 bears the marks of political struggle. On the one hand, it obliges the Bundesbank to 'support the general economic policy of the Federal Government' without prejudicing the performance of its monetary and oversight functions; on the other, it explicitly states that the central bank 'shall be independent of instructions from the Federal Government'.[13] However, no government so far has been able to make the former provision stick against that guaranteeing the Bundesbank's independence – at least not to any politician's satisfaction. This paragraph is always the reference point when there is a dispute between Frankfurt and Bonn.

Bundesbank structure

The administrative organization of the Bundesbank follows the pattern of federalism established in the Basic Law. Besides the main office at Frankfurt, there are eleven Länder central banks (LCBs), one in each of the western Länder, including Berlin and the cities of Bremen and Hamburg. Each of these supports a varying number of branch offices in the provincial cities. North Rhein-Westphalia, Baden-Württemberg and Bavaria have the largest number of branch offices (50, 38 and 32 respectively), but even Bremen and Hamburg have at least one. When the German Monetary and Economic Union came into effect, fifteen provisional Bundesbank offices were set up throughout the territory of the former GDR, with an administrative office in East Berlin headed by Bank Director Johann Gaddum. This temporary arrangement must be regularized by 1 July 1991 and will require revision of the sections of the 1957 Bundesbank Law pertaining to the Bank's organization. The consequences for the present structure are not yet clear. Several models are now under consideration in the Bundesbank, and it is possible that a rationalization will result, eliminating the smaller LCBs and increasing the number of administrative divisions at Frankfurt.

Although the Bundesbank is identified popularly with its Frankfurt Directorate, there is a strong sense of provincial pride among some LCB Presidents that there is no Bundesbank without them. Together the LCBs and their branches make up the thick net of the Bundesbank's presence across Germany, but final policy decisions are taken in the Central Bank Council (*Zentralbankrat*), which normally meets in Frankfurt. The simple addition of five new LCBs, one for each of the East German Länder, would cause a significant shift of power within the Central Bank Council and is considered unlikely at present.

(a) The Central Bank Council

The Central Bank Council (CBC) is the supreme policy-making body of the Bundesbank. Its organization follows the pattern of federal government established by the Basic Law, adhering to the federal principle of 'one Land one vote', whereby each of the Länder, regardless of its size or wealth in the Federal Republic as a whole, can cast only one vote. The Länder Central Bank Presidents, the Bundesbank President and Vice-President, and up to eight members of the Frankfurt Directorate sit on the Central Bank Council.

The Council meets fortnightly to discuss current issues and future policy. It sets monetary and credit policy for the Bundesbank, and the public announcement of these can be a news item of the first rank. Over the summer of 1988, for example, as the Bundesbank – in common with other central banks in Europe and the United States – notched up interest rates in stages of one or one-half per cent, the fortnightly meetings, and President Pöhl's press conferences afterwards, became top stories in German and international financial news. The Council's policy announcements make a public declaration of intentions and monetary will for the entire country equal to the government's economic policy decisions. It can even be argued that the Bundesbank's monetary targets constitute something like a second budget outline. Where there are conflicts over interest rates, such as occurred between Konrad Adenauer and the Bank deutscher Länder in the 1950s and between Helmut Schmidt and the Bundesbank at the beginning of the 1980s (a conflict that will be examined in greater detail in Chapter 3), the Council's policy decisions can virtually veto the economic and fiscal plans of elected German officials.

Within its own parameters, however, the Council is democratic and takes decisions according to parliamentary rules. Position papers prepared by staff in the Frankfurt Directorate and in the Länder Central Banks on domestic and international economic issues are offered for discussion at each session and the policy proposal is then put up for a vote. Proposals can also be put during the course of the meetings, and this is the usual procedure for changes in the Bank's interest rates. The politics of the Bundesbank, one of its former directors remarked, is much like politics anywhere else – a matter of persuasion and argument.

(b) *The institutional position of the Bundesbank President*
In the Central Bank Council the Bundesbank President counts for one and only one vote. Bundesbank President Karl Otto Pöhl is 'one among us' who happens to represent the Bundesbank internationally, one member of the Council commented. His institutional position, in the words of a Bank official, is 'grotesquely out of proportion to the standing Pöhl has in the arena of international economic decision-makers'. However high a Bundesbank President's international standing and 'recognition value' in public, his power to commit the Bundesbank to a particular policy in meetings of G-3 or G-7 leaders depends on the leadership skills he can exercise in the Council before and after a summit. Consensus on a particular issue can magnify the international power of a Bundesbank President, and is always necessary in getting the Bank to follow through on international agreements. Where it is missing, no amount of international goodwill can produce results, nor can the President override disagreement within the Council on an issue. Since the early 1980s, the recurrent question of how much leadership the German economy can give to the Western economies has provoked disagreement between domestic and internationalist opinion in the Council.

Political conflict of this sort went on throughout 1987 over the control of exchange and interest rates in a coordinated international system, and is likely to intensify as Germany's role in managing the international economy increases. Disagreement within the Council about the international position taken by the Bundesbank over management of exchange rates in the Plaza and Louvre agreements of 1985-7[14] and over interest rates produced a highly publicized about-face on the part of the Bundesbank in August 1987, when the

Council notched up interest rates on repurchase agreements for short-term securities on the open market from 4% to 4.25% – and provoked an angry response from the Americans. But even on such issues, the Council still works by producing an institutional consensus: whatever Pöhl might have gone into the Council arguing, the final vote was unanimous.

Viewed from the domestic side, the parliamentary function of the CBC effectively draws in LCB Presidents who without their close involvement in final decisions on policy might otherwise be more jealous of their own positions.

(c) The Frankfurt Directorate

The organizational division of the Frankfurt Directorate requires an administrative decision taken by the entire Directorate. All members must be present and no changes can be made against the President's vote. Members must be nominated by the federal government and appointed by the President of the Federal Republic. The Bundesbank Law is vague on suitable appointees, saying only that they should have 'special professional qualifications' (BBkG para. 7). Directors are normally appointed for at least eight years and may be reappointed, the average length of service being between ten and twelve years.

Like the Federal Republic as a whole, the Bundesbank has been a stable institution. So far Germany has had six Chancellors and four Bundesbank Presidents; there has been relatively little turnover in the personnel of the Länder Central Banks and Central Bank Council.

> There is no doubt [Roland Sturm has recently written] that the major aim of the provision of the Bundesbank Act which gives the members of the Central Council a period of at least eight years in office, namely to decouple the timing of the selection of top officials of the Bundesbank from the calendar of parliamentary elections, has been achieved. Newly-elected governments in the Federal Republic have never had a chance to hand the bank over to their supporters in order to secure political obedience.[15]

The main divisions in the present organization of the Bundesbank are: Treasury, Buildings, Administration and Personnel (I), headed by Dr Günter Storch; Statistics and National Economy (II), headed by Prof. Dr Otmar Issing; the International and Foreign divisions (III), headed by Dr Hans Tietmeyer; Organization and Bookkeeping (IV), headed by Ottomar Werthmöller; Banking, Minimum Reserve and the Berlin (eastern Länder) Administrative divisions (V), headed by Johann Gaddum. Credit is under the direction of Vice-President Prof. Dr Helmut Schlesinger, while Press and Public Relations and the Legal divisions and Supervision are managed by President Pöhl.

The Frankfurt Directorate runs the shop from day to day. With a staff at the headquarters of some 15,000 (6,400 civil servants and 8,600 Bank employees in varying grades), it performs a variety of administrative and analytic tasks ranging from preparation of position papers and consultative documents for internal Bank use and for Federal Ministries down to the issue of banknotes. A certain tension between Presidents of the Länder Central Banks and the Directorate is inevitable. As members of the policy-making body of the Bank (the Council), Länder Bank Presidents sometimes express a wariness towards the staff charged with execution of their policies, and can give directions to the Frankfurt Directorate as part of the institutional function of the Council. Increased market interventions by the Bundesbank, which often depend on daily and even hourly judgment of market trends, have created a particular source of tension. Such interventions are essentially executive and thus could not be exercised by such bodies as the Council. As the Bundesbank's operations in open-market transactions and its responsibilities in the management of the European Monetary System have expanded, the daily activities of the Frankfurt Directorate have also grown more important, thus widening the scope for jealousy between these two 'branches' of the Bundesbank.

(d) Länder Central Banks
Public law restricts administrative dealings with the Länder governments and transactions with local banks to the LCBs and their branch offices. The structure can claim a certain tradition in Germany, going back to the first central banking systems of the 19th century, and these Länder offices make the distribution of coins and banknotes to local banks easier. The precise organization of the LCBs varies across the Länder, but all act as the main administrative branches of the Bundesbank. Their personnel divisions and substan-

tive organization of the main offices (usually in the Länder capitals) can be schematically described as follows:

(1) *Credit* divisions administer credit operations of the LCB and supervise the branch offices' administration of the Bundesbank's interest-rate policies.

(2) *Banking* divisions supervise bank operations according to the legal regulations of the Credit Law (*Kreditwesensgesetz*) and the Bundesbank's minimum reserve policy. Reports on irregularities and the general structure of the banking industry in a particular Land are made by these divisions to the Bundesbank Directorate.

(3) The *economic* division observes and analyses general monetary and economic trends in the Land, reporting these to the LCB President in his or her capacity as a member of the Bundesbank Central Council.

(4) The *statistics* divisions collect and analyse data.

(5) A *foreign currency* division tracks investments by residents of the Land in other currencies, and those of non-residents in D-Mark investments.

(6) *Bond* divisions supervise securities transactions, and the credit needs of the Federation (*Kassenobligationen des Bunds*).

(7) Personnel, accounting, facilities management and legal divisions, common in every bureaucratic organization, also exist.

But aside from such functions, the LCBs serve as a federal anchor for Bundesbank policy-making in two ways. First and most importantly, the main offices and the branch offices act as 'listening posts' in the provinces. This aspect of their structure follows the Directorate model. They differ from the Bundesbank Directorate in having a Managing Board responsible for running the LCB on a daily basis and an Advisory Board made up of representatives of local business, banking, agricultural and labour interests. Although according to law members of the Advisory Boards are not appointed to represent their interest-groups, but to give expert advice, they clearly do function as representatives of their various economic groupings. Unlike the LCB Managing Boards, their role is purely consultative. Their effectiveness depends on the energy and imagination of the LCB President in integrating opinion from the Advisory Boards on monetary and credit policy into the decision-making process as a whole, from the Länder up to the fortnightly meetings of the Bundesbank Central Council. This varies across the CBC, with certain LCB Presidents, such as Norbert Kloten in Stuttgart and Wilhelm Nölling in Hamburg, being regarded as very skilful public opinion leaders who are able to turn technical expertise and political know-how into influence on the CBC.

The second justification for the Bundesbank's federal structure follows from the function of the LCBs as listening posts for representative public opinion. The presence of an independent and unelected body with as much power over the lives and well-being of the country's citizens as the Bundesbank seems to affront the principles of a democratic constitution. In Britain, the Chancellor of the Exchequer and the Prime Minister, both elected officials, enjoy decisive authority over the policies of the Bank of England. In the United States the Federal Reserve system is subject to Congressional review and its Chairman regularly sits before House and Senate committees on Capitol Hill and must submit a biannual report of its books to Congress. The Bundesbank is comparatively unconstrained by such constitutional arrangements, and pursues its policies formally independent of the elected officials of the West German government and the Federal Assembly, the Bundestag. In law and fact, it is Germany's monetary sovereign.

But as the economy of the Federal Republic has developed since the original Bundesbank legislation, with some Länder such as Hesse, Baden-Württemberg and Bavaria now enjoying the lion's share of the country's wealth and the northern Länder falling behind, this far-flung organization with its layers of offices and positions has come under criticism. Some believe its federal structure is now outdated, claiming that it is too big and too expensive, and that the post of LCB President has become a political sinecure for the party faithful in the Länder. Once in office, critics say, LCB Presidents have little to do but spend public money on ever-more extravagant headquarters (such as the new offices going up for the North Rhein-Westphalia LCB at Düsseldorf, and the modernization of all 22 branch offices of the LCB in Lower Saxony), or art and oriental rugs for their own offices. All this pomp and expenditure, it is claimed, is an institutional luxury that makes the LCB Presidents 'provincial princes' (*Landesfürsten*).[16]

If a federal structure really is so important for the Bundesbank, so these critics argue, then at least it should be rationalized along the lines of the US Federal Reserve Board with its twelve regional offices. If the American constitution can survive an organization that bypasses the fifty individual states in favour of administrative efficiency, surely a country no bigger than Oregon can too. In the context of European integration the tension between West Germany's federal structure and the demands of a European economy is more likely to increase than diminish, as layers of European monetary bureaucracy are superimposed on the existing organization.

A further issue is the politicization of the appointment procedure for LCB Presidents. The Basic Law allocates a particular and specific role to the political parties and thus to the federal German state, allowing for an overt politicization and a reverse flow of influence from society to the formal state structures.[17] The Bundesbank ethos demonstrates the tension between that new reality in the Federal Republic and the persistence of an older tradition of civil service expertise and loyalty to a goal above particular interests. Some observers see a gradual politicization of the Bundesbank at various levels along a scale from the Directorate (least political) to the Länder Central Banks (most political). Significant party-political inroads into the structure of the Bundesbank were made through the appointment of LCB Presidents, who in turn made appointments to the LCB Advisory Boards which followed that pattern. Several nominees for LCB President were voted down by the Central Council, only to be appointed anyway on the recommendation of a Land Minister-President. 'The fact that the Central Bank Council voted more than once against a recommended candidate', Rolf Caesar writes, 'is already an indication of the Bundesbank's politicization at the personnel level.' Even more important is the fact that the Central Council was ignored, and Caesar points to the evolution of a nominations practice for LCB Presidents that was 'regarded as theoretically possible during negotiations on the Bundesbank Law, but practically unthinkable.'[18] The most recent example of this was the appointment of the first woman to the Bundesbank. Dr Julia Dingwort-Nusseck, a popular radio commentator without any special expertise in monetary affairs, was selected as a reward for her service to the Christian Democratic Union (CDU) in Lower Saxony.

At the top of the Bundesbank, the office of President has also come under party-political influence. Karl Otto Pöhl, a member of the Social Democratic Party (SPD), was appointed by Helmut Schmidt's SPD-FDP (Free Democratic Party) government, and his reappointment under the Kohl government is regarded as a personal triumph for Pöhl. In the late 1950s Karl Blessing's appointment was widely regarded as political horse-trading; SPD Economics Minister Kurt Schiller tried to block his reappointment, but was overridden by CDU partners in the coalition.

The politics of such issues may force a revision of the current arrangement some day, but for now there are no signs of a dramatic reform in sight. None of the policy-makers at the Bundesbank believe such far-reaching independence could be sustained without a foundation in the federal structure of the LCB network. LCB Presidents are active spokesmen for the economic interests of their Länder in the CBC, a fact mentioned by Pöhl in his laudation on the retirement of Julia Dingwort-Nusseck from the Bank. Pöhl also used that occasion to remark on the importance of interest-representation in the Bundesbank Central Council: 'I think it's legitimate, and even a particular advantage of our federal and decentralized system, that the most various interests and views are expressed in the Central Bank Council . . . The federal structure of the Bundesbank is the strongest guarantee of its independence.'[19] If the Bank had a less representative function, Pöhl's public remarks suggest, its position in Germany's political system would be more likely to come under fire. A more centralized bank structure with a single office at Frankfurt would certainly be the target of greater public criticism and democratic scepticism about its special role in Germany's constitution. As a result of the currency union of East and West Germany in July 1990, the monetary administration of East Germany's transition to a social market economy, and thus much political power, has passed to the Bundesbank. In a political context shaped by fears in the East about living standards, and uncertainty in the West over the public costs of unification, the Bank's federal structure may offer an important anchor of economic and political stability.[20]

'Protecting the currency': powers and responsibilities

The key paragraph in the Bundesbank Law defines its function as 'regulating the amount of money in circulation and of credit supplied to the economy, using the monetary powers conferred on it

21

by this Act, with the aim of safeguarding the currency' (BBkG para. 3). The Bundesbank is unique among central banks in Europe and the United States in having such a definite purpose as the protection of the currency prescribed by its legislation. While legislators were precise about this purpose, however, they were less certain about how the goal was to be achieved, and this has led to endless disagreements and interpretations among commentators. Most of the political debate over the Bundesbank and its policies arises over the appropriateness of its means to that end.[21]

There have been two dimensions to the debate. The first concerns the dilemma that has dogged the Bundesbank from the mid-1950s onward: the external versus the internal value of the currency. The other focuses on the proper relationship between monetary policy and the wider goals of the general economy.

Protecting the external value of the currency
Currency stability in the meaning of the law refers to the domestic value of the mark (as measured, for example, by the basket of goods it would buy for a German household) and its external value as measured by its exchange rate against other currencies. The system of fixed exchange rates carries risks of 'imported inflation' whenever other countries' inflation rates are higher than the domestic rate. But the shift to floating rates replaced one set of problems with another, caused by large movements in currency values that were often unrelated to the fundamentals of trade flows.

Under the Bretton Woods agreement,[22] the Bundesbank sometimes resisted pressures for upward revaluation of the mark (in its first revaluation in 1961, for example, discussed in Chapter 3) on the grounds that it would make German export goods less attractive on the international markets. Throughout the 1960s and until the end of Bretton Woods, Bundesbank officials complained that their obligation to provide support for the US dollar resulted in imported inflation: strong Deutschmarks had to be put in circulation to support weak dollars, and once in the system this increased supply of money could not easily be taken out again.

When the system of fixed exchange rates broke down in 1972–3, the Bundesbank welcomed it as a relief from the pressures of market intervention and expected that floating rates would help it escape the imported inflation dilemma. This was to some extent true. The Bundesbank was helped by the development of international markets, but they also magnified its management problems, especially in the area of currency exchange rates. The Bundesbank Annual Report of 1983 referred to the large amounts of speculative inflows of foreign exchange, and the Bank began to see absorption of unforeseeable liquidity as a problem.[23] Experience with floating has confirmed the Bundesbank view, expressed in the early 1960s by its then President, Karl Blessing, and again at the end of the 1970s by President Otmar Emminger, that currency markets could not be effectively managed.

Leonard Gleske, former Director of the Bundesbank's International and Foreign divisions, has argued that the general lesson of 1980–1 and 1983 is that central bank intervention on the currency markets could have little effect, if taken in isolation from or instead of their monetary management fundamentals. If monetary growth is out of control, or where there are structural maladjustments such as balance-of-payments or budget deficits, currency market interventions have only a passing effect. In any given case, Bundesbank officials have sometimes sent the markets mixed signals. This can be part of a deliberate central bank strategy, but often it reflects differing opinion in the Bank and German government over the implications of movements in exchange rates. During the dollar's rise in May 1989, for example, with the US currency trading above the Plaza ceiling of 1.90 DM and threatening to break the G-5 agreement on its value, Bundesbank Vice-President Helmut Schlesinger called for a fall in the dollar and Finance Minister Theo Waigel agreed with American officials that 'a certain strengthening of the Deutsche Mark was appropriate'. A week later, with the dollar at 1.9888 DM, Karl Otto Pöhl said in a television interview that the German economy was not strong enough to cope with the effects of its rise.[24]

Officials today see the Bank caught between two unwelcome alternatives generated by imbalances in the US economy. Informally committed by the Plaza and Louvre agreements to a band for the dollar, the Bundesbank creates marks to buy dollars when the dollar threatens to fall below the bottom of its range. Such moves automatically increase the domestic money supply and even though the newly created marks can often be sterilized through other market transactions and it is recognized that a strong mark can limit inflationary pressures, the Bank regards these marks as a threat to monetary stability.

Dollar-market interventions can fuel domestic inflation and cause distortions in the EMS. There is thus a direct link between domestic and international economies. But the importance of the dollar and the US economy to the international economic system limits the Bundesbank's space for manoeuvre. In recent years the federal government in Germany has been more concerned than the Bundesbank that a weak dollar will erode the competitiveness of German goods in the US market. During late 1988, in conversations with the author, officials stressed the basic Bundesbank position on this, saying that intervention without control of the money supply and without a 'solid basis – interest rates in line with prices and income and the fiscal health of the economy – is bound to be ineffectual'. The message applies equally to the EMS and to the practice of Bundesbank intervention to maintain parities within its bands.

A more fundamental difference of opinion among the Bundesbank leaders can also be discerned in the debate among CBC members over the 'external security' of the mark. Both sides see *internal* stability for the mark as fundamental to the dominant paradigm of Bundesbank monetary management, but no similarly strong consensus exists on the importance of the mark's *external* value. In the Council's policy perspective, then, there is a tendency to insist on the importance of Germany's major trade partners maintaining an overall balance in the economy with comparably low inflation rates. Unless these track the German stability standard, achieving internal price stability at a constant DM exchange rate is impossible. A paradigm change is not in sight, but the underlying problems of a monetary management strategy oriented around domestic factors seem increasingly likely to cause its break-up under the pressure of external instabilities. A minority faction on the CBC, formerly led by Claus Köhler, presents the clearest challenge to a strictly monetarist priority for the Bundesbank.[25] Köhler expressed an 'unequivocal preference' for a system of fixed exchange rates and for a more active Bundesbank role in the direction of the economy well before German unification appeared as a practical item on the Bank's agenda. With unemployment set to rise in the East, and the costs of unification likely to produce more growth and inflationary pressure in the federal economy, the social issues that emerged in the 1980s as an unsuccessful challenge to the Bundesbank's anti-inflation paradigm will revive the debate in the more dramatic context of national unification.

Price stability and growth

The most difficult features of central bank money management in accordance with the provisions of the law arise in the second dimension: fitting monetary policy into a healthy relationship with the other elements in the general economy. Authoritative commentators on the Bundesbank Law see the problem as follows. Under the gold standard a single fixed point – the price of gold – provided a criterion of value external to the economic system as a whole. The gold-standard system was theoretically less complex than its successor regime, in which management of the monetary system depends on a variety of factors. The success or failure of currency management in the strict sense depends on fiscal policy, monetary policy, policy towards markets – all components of 'general economic policy' that comprises a complex of functions and relationships. As von Spindler wrote, 'although respective offices responsible for the creation of money are independent of each other, the limits to an acceptable expansion of money supply still lie in the real productive forces of the economy'.[26] By defining the goals of a central bank as it does in paragraphs 3 and 12, the Bundesbank Law creates a political field of action for the Bank: 'in the final analysis, it leaves a decision about what protecting the currency demands concretely to the central bank'.[27] Arguments over concrete applications, over the Bundesbank interpretation of what the law demands, spark the most significant conflicts between the Bank and its critics in the government and public. These conflicts have almost always been over price stability and growth.

All central banks confront some version of this problem, of course, but the combination of its legal responsibilities in the Bundesbank Law and expectations about government responsibility for growth, full employment and the balance of trade aroused by the Stability and Growth Law of 1967 makes the Bundesbank's position unique. All factions on the Central Bank Council accept the Bundesbank's primary commitment to monetary stability, but members differ on how that goal should be defined and pursued. One group has argued that an effective management strategy needs to take a wider view of stability than exclusively monetary indicators produce. The Bundesbank could more effectively control monetary pressures in the economy, so this analysis assumes, if they were measured by reference to economic potential. Such a view leads to advocacy of an active anti-cyclical strategy to stabilize the domestic economy.[28]

As the accepted framework of political economy shifted away from state intervention towards a neo-liberal approach to markets, the Bundesbank began to re-examine its policy options in the context of its legal responsibilities. The Keynesian consensus provided an organizing conception for advanced economies, a fundamental norm in their economic constitutions which in Germany was embodied in the Stability and Growth Law.[29] It came at the height of Keynesian optimism and reflected a view that 'the philosophers' stone' of economic success had been found. The formula for economic happiness contained in the Stability and Growth Law represented that optimism: it was the purpose of stability policy 'to assure price stability, full employment, and external equilibrium along with constant and appropriate economic growth in the context of a market system'. It was accepted wisdom that process-oriented thinking would eventually solve all politico-economic problems, producing both economic plenty and social peace. By contrast with that period 'the present is characterized by a lack of orientation'.[30]

A complete intellectual system with a wide-based consensus, the Stability and Growth Law was produced by the SPD/CDU coalition. Contemporaries directly involved in discussions leading up to its enactment were convinced that 'it was in near-perfect conformity with the necessity of the times'.[31] Its failure to realize its promises was not the result of inadequate information or imperfect interpretation but of 'contradictions between the constitutive characteristics of the law and fundamental facts of reality'.[32] The oil crises and the downward spiral in Western economies during the 1970s shattered the belief that economic growth could be continual and could produce a constantly increasing standard of living and new jobs.

No one still accepts the philosophy of the Stability and Growth Law today, but the law remains in effect, and fiscal debate turns on interpreting the demands of stability realistically. Neither strict monetarism nor market intervention with 'fine-tuning' defines the Bundesbank paradigm, and the internal split on the CBC is one sign of emerging uncertainty among the Bank's policy-makers over how to proceed in the new external circumstances. President Pöhl and Vice-President Schlesinger stress that the stable value of the mark made German economic success possible, and that fighting inflation remains the first priority in the Bundesbank catalogue of fiscal duties. But the rhetoric always has a particular opponent in sight – high-spending Chancellors, awkward allies, expectant domestic pressure groups. The monotonous repetition that inflation is the greatest economic disaster masks more complex thinking in the Bundesbank that offers a view of growth based on an inflation-free economy, even if it is not the Stability Law conception. Rather, constancy in economic policy, predictability, dependability and credibility are the guiding principles in the Bundesbank's approach to achieving price stability in the context of general economic goals.

Control of monetary instruments
Its legislation gives the Bundesbank four instruments of monetary policy: two interest rates, the discount rate (*Diskontsatz*), for its normal loans to other banks, and the Lombard rate (used for short-term funding and overnight bank deposits); open-market policy; and the minimum reserve policy. After the break-up of fixed exchange rates under Bretton Woods and in response to changing market conditions in general, the Bundesbank increased its use of open-market instruments and its involvement in managing the external position of the German currency on the international money markets.

Unlike some other central banks, the Bundesbank does not have direct control of interest rates or credit ceilings. It attempts to influence the markets indirectly. There are both 'long-term adjustment' and 'fine-tuning' instruments in the Bundesbank's set of policy mechanisms, although these are not always clearly distinguishable (as in the case of market transactions on repurchase agreements). Liquidity instruments aim at satisfying the banks' longer-term needs for liquidity or restraining them via these instruments. Both the Lombard and the discount rates are mechanisms designed to influence the interest-rate movements and money markets over the longer term.[33]

The Bundesbank uses bonds with short-term maturities of one week to one or two months as 'fine-tuning' devices in the market. Daily shifts of public money to the banking system, sales of short-term treasury bills, repurchase agreement transactions and sometimes foreign currency swap and repurchase transactions are all used in this way. Since the end of the 1970s these short-term transactions have been used increasingly by Bundesbank policy-makers, a sign that, despite its denials, the Bank is gradually being drawn further into the job of market management. Open-market transactions offer much greater flexibility than other central bank instruments, but they also carry much higher visibility in situations where Bundesbank activities might be read ambivalently, such as intervention (or lack of it) in the foreign-exchange markets. The most dramatic example of unwanted visibility with high unexpected costs occurred in late summer 1987. As already noted, the Bundesbank notched up interest rates on short-term issues, intend-ing to give a domestic signal. But this policy carried more weight in the international economy and intensified disagreement between US Treasury Secretary James Baker and Germany's central bank. Some analysts attribute the subsequent wave of stock-market collapses to that quarrel.[34]

A basic norm and its practice

In spite of party-political incursions into the Bundesbank, it exercises an exceptionally strong assimilative power over the most 'political' of its appointees, and it would be a mistake to think that the old tradition of public service has been lost in recent years. Rather, it survives more completely in the Bundesbank than in any other federal German institution, with the possible exception of the Constitutional Court. In the Bundesbank, as in the German civil service as a whole, the normative power of law exerts a strong influence on policy-making. The Bundesbank Law is an obvious and constant point of reference for its policy debates, and much of the concern expressed about the Bank's new international responsibili-ties centres on their compatibility with the demands of German public law. How can an institution legally bound to the 'protection of the currency' as its central task also manage the European Monetary System when other interests conflict with statutory duty? Policy-makers in the Bundesbank believe that their success with the EMS results mainly from the Bank's loyalty to its central goal. If the Bundesbank really becomes a model for a European Central Bank in the future, as the Delors Committee's *Report on Economic and Monetary Union in the European Community* seems to indicate, can other Europeans learn the German civil service tradition that is such a crucial element in its success?[35]

Those are questions for the future. For now it is safe to say that a shift away from any of the three elements in the Bundesbank ethos – protecting the external value of the currency, maintaining domestic price stability and growth, and control of monetary instruments – would amount to a revolution in the house, and would certainly be cause for a public crisis of confidence in the Bank's exercise of its constitutional obligations. The Bundesbank ethos is now very firmly rooted, able to withstand domestic and international pressures, as the next chapters will show. There are no signs that those roots are loosening, even as the international climate in which the Bundesbank acts grows stormier still.

3

THE BUNDESBANK IN THE GERMAN POLITICAL SYSTEM

The previous chapter described the Bundesbank's unique legal autonomy in the system of the Federal Republic, a characteristic some believe give it the status of a 'fourth branch' of government. Although this is not a generally accepted view, the fact that it is debated emphasizes the importance of the constitutional context of the Bundesbank for understanding its domestic position.[1] This chapter attempts to answer two questions crucial to such an understanding: first, what are the dimensions of Germany's economic constitution; and, second, how have the legal positions of the Bundesbank and federal government evolved in political practice? In other words, what makes the Bundesbank what it is today?

Economic policy and the division of powers
In every polity a formal legal arrangement of institutions and their real powers constitutes the relationship of social, economic and political forces to one another. The Federal Republic is a liberal democracy with a social market economy and a *sozialer Rechtsstaat* – a mix of social responsibilities acknowledged in law to constrain and limit the rights of individuals for the sake of a common good.[2] Its economic ground rules belong to the wider scope of law, limiting individual property rights and the rationale of profit through the concept of social rights and responsibilities. The Basic Law thus provides a foundation for Germany's national economy that is different from the political orders of more liberal economies such as the United States.

The monetary and credit powers of the Bundesbank are part of Germany's economic constitution, itself a part of the Basic Law. Its principal elements are the definition of monetary sovereignty in Germany and the definition of the Bundesbank's fundamental norm; the establishment of the relationship between the Bank and the federal government; and finally the organizational arrangement of the Bundesbank in relation to other federal agencies. The three statutory elements of the economic constitution are the Bundesbank Law of 1957, the Credit Law of 1961, and the Stability and Growth Law of 1967. The last two will be considered in their relationship to the primary legal source of the Bank's authority and powers, the Bundesbank Law.

The Bundesbank Law

Framers of the Bundesbank Law in 1957 gave weight to both aspects of a modern central bank in a democracy: regulating money creation in accordance with the powers given it in law, and accountability for that monetary policy. Their experience of the great inflation of the 1920s and of the Third Reich made the founding generation in the Federal Republic acutely aware of the consequences politicization of monetary policy could have. The Bundesbank Law incorporates checks intended to insulate the central bank from improper political pressures.[3] Public law in the Federal Republic divides the power to make fiscal policy. The Bundesbank Law assigns responsibility for general economic policy to the federal government, but it places monetary policy within the jurisdiction of the Bundesbank. This definition of institutional authorities creates the political field of the Bundesbank's activities.

The Bundesbank's monetary sovereignty in the Federal Republic is established by its statutory definition as 'protector of the currency' and by the creation of the Bank as a 'legal person *sui generis*' with a 'unique relationship, not subordinate to the Federal Government' (paras. 3 and 12, BBkG). The Bundesbank Law gives the federal government authority to determine 'general economic policy' and binds the Bundesbank to support it while also making the Bank 'independent of governmental direction' in the use of its monetary and credit powers (para. 12). This paragraph, as we have seen in Chapter 2, has been the focus of much political debate, and can be interpreted in two opposing ways: as an implicit restraint on the Bundesbank in the area of economic policy-making and as

31

authorization of its independently-determined monetary policy. The specific powers given to the federal government by other paragraphs of the Bundesbank Law imply a 'silent presumption' of governmental co-responsibility for monetary affairs, but appear to leave their relation to each other unbalanced. While the Bundesbank is independent of the government, government is responsible for the Bank's monetary policy – an arrangement that follows from the statement of a norm (general economic policy is the purview of government) and the political importance of economic decisions in a modern democratic state.

The Credit Law

The Credit Law of 1961 delegated banking supervision in Germany to the Federal Credit Regulatory Agency (*Bundesaufsichtsamt für das Kreditwesen*), an autonomous body within the Ministry of Economics. This legislation substantially enlarged the necessary coordination by Bundesbank and federal government of the whole area of credit in Germany (which is the responsibility of the Länder central banks). It also defined the boundaries of their relationship in the area of credit by giving the Federal Credit Regulatory Agency (CRA) independent policy powers over the banking industry. In cases of serious banking mismanagement which could affect the German economy, the federal government is obliged to seek the opinion of the Bundesbank. It also entitles the President of the CRA to attend meetings of the Bundesbank Central Bank Council when these pertain to the Agency's tasks.

The Stability and Growth Law

While the Credit Law defines public responsibility for supervision of banking practices, not for monetary management of credit policy, the Stability and Growth Law of 1967 raises fundamental normative issues with significant implications for economic policy in Germany. The philosophy of this law, enacted at the peak of the period of Keynesian influence, assumes that the state should intervene to ensure that inflation, trade and employment are kept in a balanced relation to one another. It accepts economic success as the criterion of governmental legitimacy and envisages the state taking on the role of guarantor for the national economy, even though state action is justified in pragmatic and limited terms.[4] As we have already seen in Chapter 2, a neo-liberal view of the proper relationship between state and society tends to be sceptical about the effectiveness of publicly organized efforts in the economic sphere and more willing to let the markets play a guiding role.

The major proponent of neo-liberalism in Germany has been the Free Democratic Party (FDP), which gained political ground during the 1980s. The two larger parties in the German system, the Christian Democratic Union (CDU) – which governs with its Bavarian sister party, the Christian Social Union (CSU) – and the Social Democratic Party (SPD), are more ideologically committed to state intervention to secure social goals than the FDP, but neither has been able to obtain a majority that would allow them to govern without a coalition partner. Disagreements over economic policy which can be traced back to their differing political philosophies caused the break-up of the SPD-FDP government under Helmut Schmidt. The Social-Liberal alliance was followed by the conservative shift of 1982. In this major realignment of political forces in Germany, as the second case later in this chapter describes, the Bundesbank played a central role.

The Council of Economic Advisers

The Stability and Growth Law also incorporated the Council of Economic Advisers into the Finance Ministry. First established in 1963 to advise the federal government on the German economy and its prospects, this Council is independent of both the Finance Ministry and the Bundesbank. Its central task is to assess the state of the German economy in an annual report to the Chancellor, and its report tends to reflect dominant economic thinking in Germany, tempered by the views of one or two outsiders. This ritual in the last fortnight of November now has an established place in the country's fiscal diary, but makes only a limited impact on economic policy-making. Although foreign observers tend to see the Council's annual report as almost equal in importance to the publication of the Bundesbank's yearly review, at home the Council carries the ironic nickname of 'the Five Wise Men' whose analyses and evaluations, according to one leading economist, have 'never seriously influenced political decisions'.[5]

The political function of the Council of Economic Advisers can be best understood as adding legitimacy to the real centre of economic decision-making through its moderate critique of the chosen path. The Five Wise Men's annual report is often criticized by the political opposition. Its 1988 Report marked the 25th anniversary of the Council and drew predictable long-range commentaries from the German press and politicians. The Social Democrats and trade unions saw its continued commitment to supply-side economics as reaffirmation of the conservative government's refusal to reduce the high level of unemployment in Germany through increased state spending.[6] The 'Alternative' Council of Economic Advisers, composed of economists closer to the Social Democrats and the German Association of Trade Unions (*Deutsche Gewerkschaftsbund*), produced a less friendly view of the government's course than their establishment counterparts. Their warning in spring 1988 that the German economy was headed for a further slowdown and their argument for a more expansive monetary course had no effect on Bundesbank policy. The real debate in autumn 1988 was not over whether to expand the money supply and state involvement in Germany, but over how much more restrictive the Bank's line should be and how quickly the markets could be liberalized.

Historical factors

Two other factors, sometimes tangent to economic policy in the federal German system, should also be noted. One is the public acknowledgment of a special responsibility towards the victims of National Socialism. This has led to substantial reparations payments (*Wiedergutmachung*) to individuals and to the state of Israel, and complicates Germany's policy towards the Middle East, constraining its dealings with the Arab states.[7] Sensitivity about the past also played a part in Germany's definition of a foreign policy towards Eastern Europe that was relatively independent of the United States during the 1970s and 1980s. Ostpolitik appeared to many West Germans as 'the long overdue break with the pre-1945 tradition of German power politics and the logical conclusion to the policies of [Germany's] reintegration of the 1950s.'[8]

The other factor is the status of a unified Germany. Between 1949 and 1990 the constitutional status of reunification shaped West Germany's policy towards the East. The Basic Law during that period treated the division as provisional and asserted the continued unitary constitutional power of the German people.[9] This constrained the Federal Republic in its foreign relations, which required that political treaties and other international agreements should be concluded with due consideration for their effect on German unity. Thus the Ostpolitik that allowed the Federal Republic to grant special credits and terms of trade to the German Democratic Republic ultimately had its rationale in the constitutional claim of national unity – a claim realized in two stages during 1990: economic and monetary union on 1 July, and formal political union on 3 October between the Federal Republic and the GDR, which thus ceased to exist as a separate state.

Summary

The impact of the structure of divided powers in Germany's economic constitution on Bundesbank policy can be summarized as follows:

(1) The activities of the Credit Regulatory Agency affect the Bank only tangentially and in extreme cases of financial mismanagement. Its predecessor was the product of the experience of banking collapse in the Depression, and the CRA is predicated on the importance of avoiding such crises by governmental oversight of the financial practices of the credit sector. The Agency is required by law to agree liquidity regulations with the Bundesbank and to manage its oversight of the German banking industry in a manner that supports Bundesbank monetary policy. With the CRA, then, the Bundesbank has a primarily *coordinating and administrative* relationship.

(2) Both the Bundesbank and the Council of Economic Advisers are concerned with national economic policy, and the personal ties between them have been close. Much of the Bundesbank's work links its members intellectually and sociologically to the same academic community from which the Council of Economic Advisers is drawn. Norbert Kloten, Land Central Bank President in Baden-Württemberg, belonged to the Council of Economic Advisers before he came to the Bundesbank, and one of the newer members of the Council, Rüdiger Pohl, studied with former Bundesbank Director Claus Köhler. Although the Council usually comments on Bundesbank policy, it has no authority over German monetary policy. Rather it can be said that, for the Bundesbank as well as for the Finance Ministry to which the Council belongs, the Council is an instrument of the necessary pluralism of expert advice modern governments must formally consult. It has no

direct relationship to the Bundesbank, which *hears its advice but is not bound by it.*

The Bundesbank and the federal government

The Bundesbank is independent of the Council of Economic Advisers and the Credit Regulatory Agency in setting monetary policy, but its relationship to the Federal Chancellor and his cabinet presents a more complex picture of the Bank's autonomy. Its legal claims to independence are enacted in a highly political field of economic policy-making on the domestic and international scene, where the autonomy of the Bundesbank looks more like the sovereignty of the state: a formal claim that cannot always be translated into practical effect.[10]

German public law frames the relations of the Bundesbank and federal government as a set of rights and duties. Although the Bank's monetary policy-making is largely autonomous of government, political leaders in Bonn do have certain powers over it. Its Directors are appointed by the Federal President on the advice of the government, and members of the cabinet are entitled to attend sessions of the Central Bank Council. Government officials have no vote in the Bundesbank central council, but they can make proposals, and the government has a suspensive veto over Central Bank Council policy. ('At [the government's] request a decision shall be deferred for up to two weeks.' – BBkG para. 13) While such a delay is not a genuine veto on the government's part, its use would send a powerful political signal to the Bank and to the political economy in Germany and the world.

The Bundesbank is legally obliged to advise government on matters of monetary policy and supply it with information as required (BBkG para. 13), and informal communication between the two goes on continuously at virtually every level. A branch of the International Division usually prepares position papers for the federal government on the funds policy of the International Monetary Fund, for example, while another provides it with continuing information on the management of the mark in the European Monetary System. But exchange of information can be an arena of political dispute, and the formal definition of the Bank's responsibilities to the elected government offers little guidance to the politics of their relationship. The currency value bands in the EMS, for example, come under the authority of the Finance Minister and federal cabinet and have been a recurrent point of contention, as we shall see in Chapter 5. The government's powers over the economy mean that the Bundesbank has less real control than it appears to have formally and must seek the consent or active participation of the government on a variety of matters ranging from nomination of the Bundesbank Directorate and the issue of small banknotes to its international obligations.

The Bundesbank has no similar institutional authority over the federal government's economic policy, but on occasion the Bundesbank's right to be consulted on proposed legislation can give it real political power over government policy, because the Bank must be informed by the government whenever major policy initiatives are planned. Debate on a draft of the Credit Law of 1961, for example, raised the question of how far the Bundesbank should be involved in the promulgation of rules under the new law. The legislature refused to give the Bundesbank a right of review and approval, because it lacks an independent power of regulation in the formal legal sense. Recognizing its material interest in credit and its regulation, however, the Credit Law of 1961 gave the Bundesbank the right to be informed and to make regulatory suggestions.

Independent of the federal government, the Bundesbank is also independent of review and control by the Bundestag, which has never questioned the Bank's position in Germany's economic constitution. Although the Bank's formulation of monetary policy often provokes domestic criticism and political controversy, this has not weakened its institutional position. Its legal status, however, engenders a degree of political power that often constrains an elected government. Although bound formally to support the government's economic policy, it has been able to assert a monopoly over the final interpretation of what 'support' in any given case means. The Bank's real power derives from its ability to make monetary policy without consulting Bonn – decisions that have an immediate impact on an electorate sensitive to fluctuations in the cost of living and on an export-dependent manufacturing sector. The two cases that follow trace the evolution of that power out of the constrained autonomy of paragraphs 3 and 12 of the Bundesbank's statutory authority.

Political practice and the evolution of power
It is generally agreed in Germany that paragraph 3 of the

Bundesbank Law accurately defines the main task of a modern central bank, but there is far less agreement on what that task requires in concrete circumstances.

Often criticized as too simplistic in its interpretation of what protecting the currency means in practice, the Bank tends to present a relatively uncomplicated picture of its job in public. When trying to justify its monetary decisions or sway political partners in Germany and abroad, the Bundesbank argues a 'strict construction-ist' line on its legal duties, stressing that preventing inflation is a necessary condition for economic growth. Asked to comment on the issue of 'growth-or-inflation', Bundesbank officials will deny there could be any real contradiction between them. Only when growth is based on sound money, they have argued consistently, can nations pursue the other goals of general economic policy – that is, full employment, stable exchange rates and balance-of-payments equilibrium.

The Bank sometimes appears to overseas observers to relegate those other goals to second place; however, internal debate about their bearing on the Bank's management of monetary policy is far more complicated. Why does so little of that complexity come across publicly when the Bundesbank disagrees with its partners in the government, or in its relations with other central banks? The story of its most intense conflicts with political leaders in Bonn provides some clues.

(a) Protecting the currency vs. economic growth, 1955–79

The first conflict between a Federal Chancellor and the German central bank came over the implications of the Bank's interest-rate policy and was one of the crucial steps towards establishing the Bundesbank in its present form. In November 1955 Konrad Adenauer tried to intervene directly in the Bank deutscher Länder's credit policies, chiding Bank President Wilhelm Vocke for taking decisions independently of the federal government at a time when 'the politics of our economic situation require that all factors work together'. Adenauer got the abrupt reply that 'far-reaching credit policy belongs to the competence of the Central Bank Council', to which the Federal Ministers for Economics and Finance were invited, and that the opportunity for consultation was always there.[11]

Six years later, as the German economic miracle was in full swing, upward pressure on the mark led to another conflict between the Bundesbank and the federal government which defined their respective spheres of power. The revaluation controversy of the early 1960s was a debate over exchange-rate policy that also carried implications for German growth. The argument then went on in language still familiar today.

After the mark went over to full convertibility in 1958, economic success combined with speculation about a possible revaluation produced a flight of capital into the German currency. The influx of foreign capital expanded the money supply and put pressure on domestic inflation rates. The situation was an entirely new challenge to the Bundesbank's efforts to prevent domestic inflation during a period of high growth. By June 1960 it confronted a choice between defending the external value of the mark and stemming domestic inflation. Chancellor Adenauer was concerned that revaluation would harm Germany's export sectors by making its goods more expensive abroad. As late as October 1960, the government opposed revaluation, and Bundesbank President Karl Blessing was fully in accord with that policy. But none of the Bank's monetary instruments – interest rates, discount policy, minimum reserves – could manage imported inflationary pressures. Rises in interest rates made matters worse by attracting more external funds. In November the Bank swung full circle, to low interest rates and monetary expansion, but was accused by the government of doing too little to fight inflation after it had reduced the minimum reserve requirements again in February 1961.

Setting exchange-rate parities is in the jurisdiction of the federal government, and Economics Minister Erhard favoured revaluation. By early 1961, however, Blessing had drawn the lines of the Bundesbank's position so tightly that the Central Bank Council had little room to move away from its opposition to revaluation. Industrial interests and Deutsche Bank President Abs also opposed revaluation. Blessing's remark that 'one shouldn't operate on a healthy currency [the D-mark] in order to cure a sick one [the US dollar]' cast the prestige of the Bundesbank publicly against a political decision to revalue the mark. But in the end the Bank lost to Bonn's political leaders, who were pushing for a modest revaluation of 5%.

When the mark was revalued, in March 1961, the Central Bank

Council abandoned its public position and voted for the government's policy – helped along by pressure from Bonn. Minister Erhard let it be known just after the Central Bank Council meeting that, had the Bank not voiced approval of a new parity, the government would have been prepared to use its suspensive veto over the Bundesbank's reduction of the minimum reserve that had just taken place.[12]

(b) Helmut Schmidt and the Bundesbank, 1981–2

The struggle between Helmut Schmidt's government and the Bundesbank over interest-rate policy which began in 1981 was the opening volley in a political conflict which eventually brought down the coalition of Social Democrats and Free Democrats that had governed Germany for more than a decade.[13] It came at a time of intense macroeconomic pressures in the international system which hit Germany particularly hard, just as it was beginning to feel the structural impact of a fading 'economic miracle'. A complicated mix of problems contributed to the clash of policies in spring 1981: the energy crisis, exchange-rate fluctuations and interest rates, and the emergence of new political alliances in the Federal Republic. This conflict between Schmidt and the Bundesbank is an especially dramatic illustration of the linkage between domestic and international pressures, and amounted to a virtual declaration of a state of emergency by the Bundesbank.

(i) The international dimension: the 1978 oil shock and US interest rates

Schmidt's conflict with the Bundesbank was set against a background of continuing energy crises in the 1970s that began with the 1973 Arab-Israeli War. For the first time the oil-dependent Western economies confronted a politically organized cartel of suppliers, and during the 1970s energy became a cause of major dislocations in the industrialized economies. Inflation combined with the depressing effect of price rises on production created something new: 'stagflation', or high inflation rates and a depressed economy. The energy crisis occurred as the Bretton Woods system was breaking down.[14] The sudden flow of capital to OPEC countries after prices rose resulted in massive reserves of petrodollars, which could not be completely invested and created major problems of management on the international exchange markets.

The established channels of international politics proved inadequate to meet these challenges in the global economy and by the mid-1970s informal initiatives to improve policy communication and coordination among the industrialized nations were under way. The most important of these was the economic summit of the Group of Seven, which had become an annual institution by its third meeting in 1977 (see Chapter 4). The first summits (1975–8) aimed at recovery from the economic shock of the first oil crisis and the end of Bretton Woods and were guided by a shared economic philosophy of demand-management.[15]

At their G-7 summits in 1979–81, Western leaders tried to agree policies on inflation and energy, but their discussions produced mainly symbolic political gestures. Until the 1981 summit the lead on international monetary policy and exchange rates was taken by France and Germany. Cooperation between Helmut Schmidt and President Giscard d'Estaing of France was especially close, and they formed a steady alliance in the European Community and at G-5 and G-7 meetings. But by the time leaders met at Ottawa in 1981, the G-7 constellation was shifting away from the approaches favoured by Schmidt and Giscard towards the neo-liberalism of Margaret Thatcher and Ronald Reagan.

For Helmut Schmidt the top items on Germany's national agenda were US interest rates, the dollar's exchange rate against the mark and the continuing energy crisis. American interest rates had risen to 21% by the end of 1980 and stayed there during the following year. The price of money in America pushed up the value of the dollar on the international markets, which rises in European interest rates could not stem. The new administration of Ronald Reagan showed little concern for the pressures these factors placed on Germany's economy, and in early 1981 Schmidt began to attack American policy, finding support from Giscard d'Estaing and from Canadian Prime Minister Trudeau and Italian Prime Minister Spadolini. The US stance had brought Germany 'the highest real interest rates since the birth of Christ', Schmidt said, and with Germany's economy already flagging and inflation on the way up, he believed high interest rates would only worsen his country's position.[16] François Mitterrand, Giscard's successor, was sympathetic to the Germans. He came into office in May 1981 promising to revive the French economy and create jobs, and had nothing to gain politically from high bank rates. Together the French and German heads of government planned to find a way out of the American straightjacket.

(ii) The end of the fat years: the German predicament in 1981
The German government's budget deficit for 1980 – 28 billion marks, or 1.82% of GDP – was the biggest in thirty years and the largest in the Western world. There was a trade deficit of 25 billion marks. Inflation was high by German standards at 5.5%, as was the Lombard rate at 9%.[17]

At the start of 1981 the Bundesbank faced the conflicting claims of monetary stability versus economic growth – complicated by other factors, such as energy conservation and wages and prices policy. During the spring, institutional conflict with the federal government added another dimension to the elements of the domestic-international divide. The Bundesbank faced a coalition that was itself deeply divided over Germany's fiscal policy; the strains of a twelve-year stretch of governing together were beginning to show. Schmidt's view of the situation was clear and relatively simple: American interest rates compounded the difficulties caused by the second oil shock. The only way out was a combination of new energy sources and the reduction of bank rates.

Worrying as the oil shock was, its effects were intensified by Schmidt's other political problems at home. By 1981 the German ecology movement was a force at the local level, although the Green Party did not achieve its parliamentary breakthrough until the January 1983 national elections. Citizens' initiative groups *(Bürgerinitiativen)* all over Germany organized grass-roots opposition to the development of atomic power and industrial expansion. A new runway on the west side of Frankfurt Airport became the scene of pitched battles in early 1981, and, fearing more violence, the government appealed to demonstrators to stay away. A chronic shortage of housing produced massive 'squats' in the largest German cities, and in university towns there were dramatic clashes between masked demonstrators and police in riot gear. In that environment, some of the worst elements of the old Germany also seemed to reappear. When the conservative government of Bavaria detained youthful demonstrators for days without charge, the cover of one German weekly voiced what many people feared: 'Is the *Rechtsstaat* in danger?'[18] Domestic tensions were heightened by the

NATO plan to station American cruise missiles in Germany. As the doctrine of 'mutual assured destruction' lost credibility, new short-range missiles were part of Helmut Schmidt's plan to tie the Americans to European defence. But even before the new weapons arrived, the German public was agitated about them. Unwilling to be the battleground of East-West conflict, younger Germans especially regarded the rhetoric of the cold war and Schmidt's world view as anachronistic.

Just on the horizon, too, were issues beyond Schmidt's pragmatic approach. Questions about the legitimacy of liberal democracy and the quality of life in a consumer society preoccupied a younger generation of Germans. Although far less radical than terrorist groups of the late 1970s such as Baader-Meinhof, the leaders of Germany's emergent 'eco-peace' movement were also a product of the 1968 student revolt. They believed that only if the Federal Republic changed the consumerist mentality that had shaped the years of its economic miracle could a balance between nature and society be restored.

Discord over defence policy, energy policy and Germany's industrial structure increased internal pressures in the SPD. At the same time trade unions in the Federal Republic were about to enter into a new round of wage negotiations and, with unemployment rising, they pressed the SPD side of the coalition to stimulate domestic demand in precisely those traditional areas of industry that were big energy consumers. German workers, who already enjoyed the highest wages in Western Europe, entered the wages negotiations demanding that their new pay scales should exceed the rate of inflation by at least 3%.

The SPD's coalition partners in the FDP were beginning to pull in a different direction. Count Otto Lambsdorff, then Economics Minister, was especially critical of his partners in government, and anxious to make budget cuts that could scarcely be accepted by the SPD's trade-union constituency. Although the FDP had committed itself to getting taxes down, there seemed little room to do so with the budget in deficit. Even though private savings were very high at 15%, the general climate for new ventures was decidedly bleak. The Free Democrats doubted that government action to stimulate growth could be effective. These conflicts unsettled the coalition, adding to the pressure on Schmidt's electoral base. By early 1981, with new social movements challenging his style of government and the SPD's left wing restive about German defence policy, the Chancellor's position had become severely weakened. Into that situation stepped the Bundesbank with a dramatic rise of interest rates.

(iii) *Closing the 'Lombard window': the Bundesbank intervenes*

When Germany's central bankers met in the third week of February 1981, the mark had been under constant downward pressure on the exchange markets for a month. Its trade-weighted index fell 15 points over a year and a half and the dollar stood at 2.16 marks in New York. The unusually high Lombard rate (9%) had already put German business under pressure. Rising unemployment meant that medium-sized and family firms with relatively narrow capital bases found it difficult to secure finance for new ventures they could normally exploit in the downtown of the business cycle. The Bundesbank's policy dilemma had some familiar elements, such as the danger of 'imported inflation' caused by a weak mark, but it was complicated by 'stagflation' in the German economy.

Speculation about the Bank's course built up in anticipation of its usual Thursday session and there was agreement that its position was extremely difficult. An increase in rates seemed necessary for exchange-market reasons, but could saddle the Bundesbank with the blame for a recession. If the Bundesbank did nothing, the *Financial Times* commented, 'its commitment to defend the currency will be thrown into doubt'.[19]

Although some increase in the Lombard rate was expected, the Bank's decision at that Thursday meeting (19 February) caught everyone off-guard. The Central Bank Council voted to put up the basic rate by a maximum of three full points, raising the cost of central bank money to the German banking industry from 9% to 12% with immediate effect. It also declared what amounted to a state of emergency in Germany's monetary and credit system, sharply reducing liquidity available to the banks and increasing its own room for manoeuvre with four steps:

(1) Commercial banks' access to overnight funds through Lombard was suspended;

(2) A 'special Lombard rate' for short-term credit was introduced, forcing banks to obtain the necessary liquidity at rates that would vary daily;

(3) The amount of credit available under the 'special Lombard' system was also variable on a daily basis;
(4) Banks were told to repay immediately their existing credits under the normal Lombard system – an estimated 6.5 billion DM.

At the same time, the Bundesbank announced continued interventions on the money markets through open-market transactions and repurchase agreements. For banks which found themselves in debit at the end of a business day, the Bundesbank would make 'special Lombard' provisions, but the credit thus obtained had to be repaid on the next day.

Meeting the press to announce the Central Bank Council's decisions, Karl Otto Pöhl declared that the Bundesbank had 'no alternative, even if we wanted' to the new flexible system of Lombard credits. 'A deficit country cannot afford a policy of low interest rates', Pöhl asserted, trying to shift the blame for the Bank's decisions firmly back into the government's court. High interest rates were the unavoidable consequence of a deficit and currency devaluation. Low interest rates could only be expected if Germany's 'stability advantage' was regained; monetary policy must not be used to pursue extraneous economic goals and the Bank offered some unasked-for advice to Bonn on sensitive domestic issues. In spite of the difficult situation existing at the time, there should be no reversal of fiscal policy. Wage demands in the current round of negotiations were explicitly mentioned as a factor contributing to Germany's difficult external position. Speaking on behalf of the Bundesbank's policy-making council, Pöhl also warned that the Federal Republic 'could not allow itself the luxury of abandoning atomic energy'. Everything must be done, he concluded, to reduce the long-term costs of industrial production, and there was no practical alternative to atomic power.

The markets' immediate reaction to the Bundesbank's new policy was confused. The cost of Euromoney went up to 11% in Frankfurt that afternoon. In London the dollar fell more than five pfennigs against the mark, compared to the previous day's trading, to 2.1340 DM, and it was down 12 pfennigs over the week's starting figures (2.25 DM). The mark rose against the French franc in its EMS band. German bankers showed predictable scepticism about the Bundesbank policy. Dr Wilhelm Christians, co-chairman of the powerful Deutsche Bank, said the new system would inevitably place strains on the commercial banks and emphasized that higher interest rates would not cure stagflation.

The government in Bonn saved its anger for the Americans. Helmut Schmidt, in an interview in *Le Monde*, called US interest rates 'destructive' and 'absolutely unacceptable if we are still to pursue the aim of full employment'. Two domestic political factors intruded into the discussion during the week. First, a lower court banned the planned demonstration at the Brockdorf atomic power plant and the Bonn government appealed to demonstrators to stay away. Four years earlier hundreds of people had been injured at Brockdorf and government officials were concerned that the violence would be repeated. The plant, a joint project of Schleswig-Holstein's Christian-Democratic government and the SPD government of Hamburg, symbolized the domestic political tensions now beginning to emerge. Then, a day before Schmidt spoke to *Le Monde*, the Bundesbank's Vice-President, Helmut Schlesinger, warned of the consequences of excessive pay rises in the current round of negotiations. Although Schlesinger was not speaking officially for the Bundesbank in stating that he favoured a temporary freeze on pay in Germany, his comments were widely seen as an indication of the Bank's concern over developments in the economy as a whole. The government seemed unable to moderate labour demands in the pay dispute, and one of the largest unions, IG Metall (the metal workers) held out for 8% against the industry's offer of 2.5%.

In the domestic context the Bundesbank's actions seemed exaggerated. There were signs that the German public worried more about recession and unemployment than inflation, and the Bank's position on energy policy also seemed out of touch with a vocal portion of German public opinion, only complicating the government's difficulties on that issue. Measured by the Bundesbank standard of stability, however, these were comparatively minor worries: the cost of 'daily money', or overnight credit available to the banks under the 'special Lombard' system, went up to 28% a week after the Central Bank Council meeting on 19 February. In a public display of political pressure, a delegation of SPD politicians called on Pöhl the following week. Finance Minister Hans Matthöfer called for a cut in international rates, while Economics

Minister Otto Lambsdorff remarked coolly that while such a move would be helpful, it was unrealistic to expect it.

Tensions in the governing coalition were evident when the conservative *Frankfurter Allgemeine Zeitung* took up the Bundesbank's position on 14 March, shifting the national debate onto lines which, when the SPD-FDP coalition fell eighteen months later, would define the new points of political orientation for the German economy. Depicting the domestic controversy over unemployment versus inflation as one that affected the entire future of the Federal Republic, the *Frankfurter Allgemeine* outlined the basics of a neoliberal position that already formed the basis of both Mrs Thatcher's policy and that of Ronald Reagan. The question of 'supply-side' economics now leaped to the top of Germany's national agenda. Urging the Bundesbank to 'remain firm', the *Frankfurter Allgemeine* described policy debate in the Bank as 'more difficult now than at any time in the postwar period. The Bundesbank should not let itself be swayed from this course regardless of its dangers. One wants to say to Pöhl – remembering Luther – "Little monk, you have a hard road to follow".'[20]

Over the next few weeks, the Bundesbank bolstered its position in public, defending the tough stand on interest rates, and warning that high wage settlements threatened the German economy more than the cost of borrowing. IG Metall seemed to move slightly from its position, dropping its demands from 8% to 4.5%, and as the exchange markets settled down and accustomed themselves to the new Lombard system, the mark rose against the dollar, trading at between 2.0320 and 2.056 in Frankfurt. Within the EMS the mark regained its place as the strongest currency, and the Bundesbank no longer needed to intervene to support it. Trying to keep up momentum, Pöhl even remarked that he expected a revaluation soon, and again asserted that although the Bundesbank course would mean 'hardship and sacrifice', the Bank's first obligation was to defend the value of Germany's currency.

By the first week of April, the objectives of Bundesbank policy seemed to have shifted. Worry about the mark's international value had initially justified its dramatic moves in late February, but other economic goals now appeared to dominate Bundesbank thinking. Schlesinger's critique of the unions' wage demands continued, as did Pöhl's public reiteration of the Bundesbank standard. The government showed no sign of closing its deficit, and a prominently placed analysis of 'the pitfalls of deficit financing' (*Abschnittsfinanzierung*) in the *Frankfurter Allgemeine* turned public attention towards the increased costs of the public debt. 'The state hardly has an alternative in arranging its credit: its deficit has to be financed at the market's rates.'[21]

(*iv*) *Going to the Saudis: Schmidt tries to circumvent the Bundesbank*
Under growing political pressure, the Chancellor called a meeting of senior Ministers and Bundesbank officials in Bonn on 2 April. At the top of Schmidt's agenda was the question of how to get the German economy moving again, and he hoped to generate a consensus among government and Bundesbank officials as the basis for an effective public announcement. There was a hopeful sign from the Munich-based Institute for Economic Research (IFO), which reported a decrease in unemployment and a slight improvement in overseas demand for German goods to compensate for a continuing drop in domestic orders. Meeting in its regular Thursday session the day before, the Bundesbank central council signalled no changes, however, in its tight-money policies. So when the Frankfurt bankers came to Bonn the next day, they could offer the government little by way of new gestures.

By all accounts their meeting was stormy, with Schmidt demanding a reduction of interest rates and telling Pöhl and Schlesinger they were interfering in the rightful sphere of government business. Unless the Bundesbank changed its line, it would undermine the legitimate decisions of his government on energy policy, unemployment and the business cycle. The German public would not stand for that, Schmidt asserted, and were demanding even more than he was prepared to do. The bankers repeated their position throughout the long session which lasted until past midnight.

On the next morning Schmidt's press officer, Kurt Becker, announced the outlines of a new package of measures to stimulate the economy and encourage investment in alternative forms of energy. The government's aim, Becker told the press, was to reduce the German deficit by bringing down the country's energy costs. In addition to the strains high energy costs had placed on the government's budget, Employment Minister Ehrenberg noted that unemployment was costing Germany's social insurance fund an extra 4 billion marks. The high cost of borrowing also added to the deficit, the government said; these additional public burdens, combined with increased defence costs in the wake of the new missile deployment, would increase the deficit by a further 6 to 10 billion marks. This public explanation of the government's difficulties was an oblique attack on the Bundesbank, which had now replaced the Americans in Schmidt's eyes as the root of his problems. But he had also played an extraordinary hand in his meeting with Pöhl and Schlesinger. Before entering the meeting, Schmidt agreed a joint financial strategy with French President Giscard d'Estaing. The two leaders had worked closely together and felt they knew how the European Community should evolve: the motor of European politics was German economic power and French political nous. They had taken the first important step towards monetary unification before the second oil shock by establishing the European Monetary System. Now international events threatened to reverse the progress they had made in the 1970s. Added to that, Giscard was facing election that spring and it was not clear whether he would hold onto power in France. Schmidt was anxious to help his old friend and unhappy about the strains German monetary policy was placing on the French government. Just before an election was no time for the French franc to be coming under pressure in the EMS, however well that suited the Bundesbank's medium-term strategy for stability. Giscard was equally aware of Schmidt's domestic troubles in the spring of 1981.

Together they came up with a plan to help each other out of the political clinch, and one that contributed to solving the urgent problems of energy. It would even do something to recycle OPEC's petrodollars and help flagging Western economies. The French and German governments would extend their borrowing from the OPEC countries during the coming economic year. Bonn had already accumulated debts of 6 billion marks (5.5 billion of it from Saudi Arabia) the previous year in credits arranged through commercial banks. When private funds were counted, Bonn's total indebtedness in the preceding year doubled to 12 billion DM. Early in 1981, Horst Schulmann, State Secretary in the Finance Ministry, went to Riyadh to negotiate credits for the 1982 fiscal year. Schmidt and the French Prime Minister, Raymond Barre, had agreed the details of the package on the morning of Schmidt's meeting with Bundesbank officials. The French, with their parliamentary elections scheduled for May, wanted only a speedy conclusion to the arrangement.[22]

When details of the financial plan were presented to Pöhl and Schlesinger on 2 April, they balked. Not only could there be no immediate reduction in Bundesbank rates or end to the 'special Lombard' system, the Bundesbank would not cooperate with the Saudi deal through the issue of new federal bonds. Schmidt contacted the French soon after the meeting to tell them that the project was now in doubt, and encouraged French criticism of Germany's central bank, which he himself attacked the following weekend. In a conversation with reporters the same weekend, Prime Minister Barre blamed the Bundesbank for much of Europe's fiscal misery. He claimed that the Bank's interest-rate policy, not the government in Bonn, had caused the economic recession that was also beginning to affect France. Barre also confirmed rumours that he had written to Schmidt proposing joint Franco-German action to cut interest rates.

Observers in Bonn saw the conflict between government and the central bank increasingly as an institutional crisis: Schmidt's plans to give interest-rate subsidies to firms that invested in energy programmes no longer seemed a purely economic scheme, but a signal to the Bundesbank. The assumption of credits from oil-producing nations would be used to subsidize investment by medium-sized firms in the energy sector and would be 'aimed at protecting the economy from the effects of high interest-rate policy', Parliamentary Chairman Hoppe said. The German economics institutes joined the fray, with criticism of all concerned: government, Bundesbank, the unions and industry were all failing to manage the Germany economy. The Bundesbank, IFO warned, was in danger of 'overkill' on interest rates.

(v) Who defends the currency? Bonn loses to Frankfurt
By mid-April the lines of an implicit constitutional conflict were drawn. After the Bundesbank leaders rejected his financing plans, Schmidt's government found a loophole in the law that regulated their relations. Had the financial arrangement proceeded according to plan, the Bundesbank would have issued new bonds which the OPEC creditors would have bought. When the bank refused on the grounds that it meant an unacceptable increase in the money supply, the Franco-German scheme seemed to be doomed. But Saudi money could be channelled through the Credit Agency for Reconstruction (*Kreditanstalt für Wiederaufbau*), a legislative left-over from the

1950s, without action by the Bundesbank. Acting as a middleman for the government, this agency would borrow the money and administer it for two purposes: extra capital for government investment plans, and interest subsidies for energy investment. The demonstration of Franco-German harmony on economic policy, a symbol of the ability of both governments to manage their flagging economies and do something about the inflationary costs of energy, could proceed.

Formally nothing prevented the German government from solving its dilemma in this way, and its strategy might have been ingeniously successful against a central bank with less autonomy or one less well established in its native political culture. As things turned out, the government's plan threw the legal-political dimensions of the central bank–governmental relationship in the Federal Republic into sharp relief. The conflict between Schmidt's government and the Bundesbank demonstrated the importance of Germany's legal culture in an economic crisis. The clash also underlined the importance of politics to the outcome of any conflict over interpretation in a concrete situation. In this conflict, both functions of the state's sovereignty were at stake: who makes foreign policy, and who authorizes the currency? This was a struggle for political power at the obvious level. The SPD was already in electoral trouble and after twelve years in power it had begun to look stale and weary of governing. Only Schmidt's personal popularity and his high standing as a world statesman held things together. At a deeper level, however, first principles of Germany's economic constitution were on the line. Paragraph 3, enjoining the Bank to protect the currency, seemed inconsistent with the injunction of paragraph 12 that the Bundesbank support government policy. Who decided which had precedence? What were the limits of paragraph 12 obliging the Bank to support the government's general economic policy, and how could they be determined? It was a matter of judgment, and for the next few months both sides manoeuvred to claim legitimacy for their view.

When the Bundesbank's 1980 Annual Report appeared in the spring of 1981 it contained an explicit rebuke for government policy. Germany, the central bankers said, had been 'living beyond its means'. If the government tried to stimulate the economy, it warned, the necessary economic adjustment would be all the more painful. The report was widely read as an attack on Schmidt's financing plans, and warned Germans they were in danger of frittering away the substance of postwar recovery if the government pursued its course. The balance of Germany's reserves was sinking rapidly: from 109.5 billion marks in 1978 to 61.5 billion at the end of 1980 – a reduction of 48 billion marks, which the Bundesbank attributed to Germany's 40 billion mark budget deficit for 1979 and 1980.[23] Taking up a position in direct conflict with government, the Bundesbank urged completion of Germany's atomic energy programme as the best way to secure the country's future energy needs and restore the Federal Republic to its competitive advantage over other exporters.

As a poor showing on its balance-of-payments account turned up in May, and the mark continued to lose value against the dollar, Bundesbank Vice-President Schlesinger repeatedly attacked the government's foreign borrowings. Public expenditure cuts would have to be made, he warned, or the situation would worsen. At a meeting of the World Congress of Savings Banks at the end of May, the President of the Federal Republic, Francis Carstens, took sides with the Bundesbank, telling the delegates that inflation helped no one in the long run. That message was reinforced by Pöhl, who declared that the Bundesbank had never been willing to make up for economic mistakes by reshaping its monetary policy, nor would it do so now. High interest rates would come down when Germany's budget was back in order. Speaking a fortnight later, just before the budget debate in the Bundestag, Pöhl made an even more direct attack on the government:

> The crisis in which we find ourselves may have its good side. Perhaps it will help those it affects to realize how serious the situation is ... In many corners of society, the change in our economic circumstances has not been fully accepted. One has gone along as though everything remained the same. But gradually it seems to be dawning on people that you can't ignore objective constraints and you can't get rid of economic facts by ignoring them. It's a cheap strategy to make the Bundesbank a whipping boy for all these failures and omissions ... Developments on the markets over the last few days signal something like a crisis of confidence which we cannot simply accept ... Creating the necessary trust in our currency is a very practical political task and one which the Bundesbank ought

not to be abandoned in pursuing. The public must do something, as must the state with its expenditure plans and negotiation partners in the round of pay agreements.[24]

Two weeks later, as the bond and equity market in Germany improved, Pöhl was more optimistic about the budget deficit. He was also encouraged by the pay settlements: all the big unions had come around to 5%, a figure that he remarked was 'exemplary by international standards'. A fortnight after that, the Central Bank Council again tightened its monetary policy, declaring that it would aim towards the bottom range of its corridor of 4–7% for 1981. The same week, a special report by the Council of Economic Advisers urged Bonn to cut its spending plans. This added another voice to that of the Bundesbank in opposition to the coalition's plans.

In the political struggle over Schmidt's fiscal policy, the Bonn government found itself outflanked. Although it tried to mobilize public fears of unemployment and redirect the blame for Germany's difficult economic position towards the central bank, that strategy failed. Giscard's government lost the French elections of May 1981, and even though Mitterrand was equally interested in the joint Franco-German loan, the project was already badly off the rails. During debate on the next year's budget, Finance Minister Matthöfer suggested that the government's deficit could be plugged by taking money from three sources: the Bundesbank's foreign reserves; the increased income the Bundesbank could expect from interest on its dollar holdings; and Bundesbank profits from its credits to German banks.

By midsummer, time had run out for the SPD-FDP coalition in Bonn. Although Schmidt's government soldiered on until September, tensions over spending and taxes came out in the Bundestag debate on the 1982 budget. The FDP refused to accept an SPD plan for a surtax to finance programmes to fight unemployment, and finally forced the coalition's break-up, shifting to a new government under Helmut Kohl's Christian Democratic Party. The FDP line ran perfectly parallel to that of the Bundesbank. Speaking to an American journalist in early August 1981, Pöhl remarked: 'The Social Democrats feel ... you can't cut spending, particularly for welfare, without doing something for jobs. I'm of the opinion that a surtax and spending programme would be completely counter-productive. What we need are improved exports and a reduction in

53

the current-account deficit. Reducing the deficit will improve the job market over the long run.'[25]

Conclusion

The Bundesbank's battle with Helmut Schmidt's government demonstrates how it can wield political power through use of its monetary policy instruments. Its predecessor, the BdL, in its early conflict with Konrad Adenauer, was able to assert its authority quickly, thus contributing to a tradition of central bank independence in the Federal Republic. The revaluation controversy of 1961 produced more mixed results for the Bundesbank, partly because of its own indecisiveness on the issues. What are the implications of these cases for assessing Bundesbank behaviour in the politics of the Federal Republic?

(1) The Bank is willing to transgress the line dividing the government's rightful sphere of 'general economic policy-making' from its own area of monetary responsibility when its chances of winning against a relatively weak opponent seem good.

(2) Bundesbank rhetoric stresses its duty to 'protect the currency', but legal norms have to be enacted in political practice. Its interpretation of the Bank's legal rights and responsibilities was effective in 1981–2 because its policy coincided with those of a decisive parliamentary actor in Bonn, the Free Democrat Party. Without a parliamentary ally of that stature, it is unlikely that the Bank would challenge an elected government so directly.

(3) The Bundesbank is in a better position than governments to pursue its policies by reference to German constitutionalism because its claims to expert objectivity can be more easily translated into concern for the common good than similar claims by politicians. Bonn can nudge the Bank on monetary policy but open challenges to its institutional prerogatives or attempts to circumvent its power to control money supply are bound to fail.

(4) Although there is evidence that the political realities which gave birth to the Bank's legal brief as Germany's monetary sovereign – widespread fear of inflation throughout the

populace – have changed, there are no signs that the Bundesbank Law or the Bundesbank standard is about to shift with the times. Elected governments will have to come to terms with the Bank's independent interpretation of its statutory duties for the foreseeable future. As we have seen, that can impose significant constraints on political manoeuvrability.

In conclusion, one can say that the story of the Bundesbank's evolution in the German political system has been a model of institutional success; there are no serious domestic threats to its position, nor has the monopoly of its interpretation of what 'protecting the currency' requires of Germany's government and people been effectively challenged in the EMS era. Bundesbank policy-makers can look sanguinely towards Bonn; but their view of the rest of the world, as we shall see in Chapter 4, is very different.

4

THE BUNDESBANK IN THE INTERNATIONAL ECONOMIC SYSTEM

The stock market crash of 1987 began with a family quarrel. The Germans, US Treasury Secretary James Baker complained during a television interview on 17 October, were doing too little to expand their economy and too much to control inflation. Current monetary policy in the Bundesbank, Baker asserted, was undermining international agreements on exchange rates and an internationally agreed strategy for coordinating economic policy by the G-7. If the Bundesbank didn't fall into line, he warned, the deal over monetary policy reached by the G-7 at the Louvre was off: the US would let the dollar, which had already lost 14% of its value against the mark over the preceding year, fall even further.

On the following Monday, 19 October, after five years of a bull market, stock exchanges in New York, London and Tokyo experienced what New York Stock Exchange Chairman John Phelan called 'a financial meltdown', and officials in Washington and New York considered closing the largest of the American exchanges until investors' nerves calmed.[1] US trade figures had revealed an unexpectedly high deficit the week before ($15.7 billion), and that had already started the fall in stock prices. But now they virtually collapsed. When the exchanges reopened the Monday after Baker's attack on the Germans, the glimpse of a rift in the carefully crafted strategy of G-7 coordination was enough to send equity prices tumbling. In a single day the Dow Jones lost 508 points, or 23% of its opening value. It was a far greater loss than the 13% fall on the New York Stock Exchange in 1929 that marked the beginning of the great depression.

Neither the Americans' irritation nor the Germans' stubbornness should have surprised anyone who followed economic diplomacy. Tension over interest rates and supply-side economics had been building up since the middle of the previous year, when Baker launched his first sharp attack on the interest-rate and money-supply policies of the Bundesbank.[2] The Germans' first priority was keeping inflation at its record 1986 low and slowing growth in their money supply. The Americans wanted growth rates in Europe up to stimulate demand for American imports and help reduce the American trade deficit. Primary national interests were at stake – and in conflict with each other.

In the domestic setting, as Helmut Schmidt's conflict with the Bundesbank during 1979–82 illustrates, minimizing inflation and protecting the value of the mark will take priority over other, conflicting, economic goals. In the broader pattern of Bundesbank–government relations, the effect of the Bundesbank's policy paradigm is to set monetary stability against other economic goals, such as growth and full employment, at times of fundamental conflict over the direction of the domestic economy. What happens when the Bundesbank faces similar choices in the international area? What arguments are pursued? How much autonomy does the Bundesbank have there – or, to put it another way, how dependent is Germany's central bank on foreign policy decisions taken elsewhere?

German monetary policy to the end of Bretton Woods

Although the sources of external pressure on the mark have changed over the past thirty years, the Bank's primary target has been 'imported inflation', and its experience in those early years is still used to justify its policies. It is as well, then, to set out the main lines of these policies before turning to the Bundesbank's view of its exposed flank today.

German monetary policy has to aim at two sometimes incompatible goals, as Bundesbank policy-makers see it: protecting the domestic purchasing power of the currency, and stabilizing the external value of the mark. The global factors defining the Bank's policy situation emerged clearly in the conflict between Helmut Schmidt's government and the Bundesbank, as we have seen in Chapter 3, but in the Bundesbank's view the fundamental issue has not changed since the late 1950s: a balance-of-payments disequilibrium aggravated by speculative inflows of foreign currency. 'Since the mid-50s,' former Bundesbank President Otmar Emminger wrote, 'German stabilization policy has repeatedly been undermined by influences originating abroad. In no other major country has imported inflation played such a major role as in the Federal Republic of Germany.'[3] This seemed less of a problem to foreign observers, who saw the strong Deutschmark as reducing inflationary pressures. The problem for post-Bretton Woods economies was different. Exchange-rate fluctuations were so great that they distorted the domestic economy over the medium term, swinging from overvalued to undervalued levels, with consequences for output and inflation.

The other factor was foreign political pressure on Germany to 'do more' in carrying the burden of the world's economy. This was a key political issue in Helmut Schmidt's 1981 conflict with the Bundesbank, and the clash of interests that preceded the crash of October 1987 can also be defined in these terms. From the Bundesbank's perspective, both elements appear as disruptive forces in its management of the currency, and much of the policy debate throughout the Bank's history has focused on minimizing the damage external factors could do to stable currency values.

Over the period from 1948 to 1975, the strength of German exports exposed the Bundesbank goal of internal stability to repeated stresses. When the Deutschmark was created in 1948, Germany entered the international economy as a deficit country without foreign currency reserves. In less than a decade, as official statistics shown in the tabulation below demonstrate, the situation was reversed. Buoyant external demand for German-manufactured goods created persistent trade surpluses between 1951 and 1961, and in summer 1957 these led to the first large speculation on a revaluation of the German currency.[4]

The economies of the United Kingdom and France profited from

Balance of trade in the FRG (DM billion)

1949	−0.3	1956	+5.0
1950	−0.3	1957	+6.5
1951	+2.5	1958	+6.6
1952	+2.7	1959	+4.8
1953	+4.1	1960	+5.6
1954	+4.0	1961	+4.0
1955	+2.7		

the Korean War boom as Germany did, but showed much more rapid inflation. Despite the Bundesbank's efforts to stem the inflow of foreign capital through lower interest rates and a direct ban on interest payments for foreign deposits, foreign exchange flowed into Germany during the first nine months of 1957. Speculation about a revaluation aggravated the internal position of the mark, which was already running a surplus – a position which only eased with the 1957–9 world recession. As speculative inflows reversed, fiscal recession served the ends of monetary stability, a process the Bundesbank welcomed. Slower external demand for German goods also cooled the domestic economy, laying the foundations for more solid growth (in the Bundesbank's view) and making it less suscep- tible to inflationary pressures:

> With the disappearance of the long-persisting pull on exports ... a situation is arising in which the previously almost unbridgeable conflict between the requirements of internal monetary stability and those of balance-of-payments equilibrium might be resolved. The slackening of exports has widened the margin for a non-inflationary expansion of the domestic economy.[5]

During the first revaluation debate, the Bundesbank opposed the government's economic policy, but in 1961 it lost the argument to Economics Minister Ludwig Erhard, who favoured an increase. Although most commentators thought the 1961 revaluation was too little and too late, there were no new crises for the German mark despite the fact that 1962–7 were turbulent years for the world economy as a whole, with pronounced exchange-rate pressures in Italy, the Netherlands, France and Britain.[6]

As a leading exporter, Germany depends on favourable exchange rates for the mark, especially relative to the dollar. If the mark rises too sharply against the dollar, that affects the capacity of German industry to sell its products in the United States, and in other countries whose incomes are dollar-sensitive, such as OPEC. The profits of German exporting industries are correspondingly vulnerable to fluctuations in the exchange-rate system. If, on the other hand, the dollar rises too sharply against the mark, Germany's economy is hit in its other sensitive spot, the cost of raw materials, especially oil. Price rises in this sector produce a ripple effect on domestic prices.

The external value of the mark and sensitivity to foreign demand for its goods created Germany's central dilemma, a situation which Bundesbank policy-makers saw as compounded by fixed exchange rates. The formal obligation to buy and sell dollars and marks under the Bretton Woods system generated additional monetary management problems. The lack of external security meant that 'German monetary policy was disturbed over a long period of time by interest rate induced and speculative inflows of capital' and 'finally had to limit itself to endeavouring to neutralize the expansive influence from abroad by contractive processes at home'.[7]

The end of Bretton Woods removed the constraint of obligatory intervention to support official exchange rates. With its external flank secured, the Bank was free to develop its post-1973 paradigm: priority for domestic stability and constancy in monetary policy. But this period of relative international independence was short-lived. The introduction of the European Monetary System on 13 March 1979 placed new intervention responsibilities on the Bundesbank, ultimately creating a European Bretton Woods with the German currency as anchor. Nor could the Bundesbank ignore the dollar even after Bretton Woods. During the 1980s the dollar's rise and fall introduced new instabilities into the world economy which could be checked only by agreement among the major economic powers.

By the crisis year of 1987 these factors had revived the old problem of an exposed external flank for Bundesbank policy-makers. Internationally committed once again via the Plaza and Louvre agreements, as well as the EMS, the Bundesbank standard continued to guide policy through the turbulence of the late 1970s and the 1980s, a period when the Germans came under increased pressure to take a greater economic lead.

Interregnum: the German locomotive, 1976–8
The yearly economic summit of Western heads of government and finance ministers had become an institution with a patchy record of achievements by the late 1980s. The gathering of G-7 leaders grew out of a closed diplomatic session initiated in 1974 by France and Germany. The original idea, Helmut Schmidt later remarked, was 'a private informal meeting of those who really matter in the world' and the early summits were modelled on the 'Library Group' that met in the White House for the first time in April 1973.[8]

Schmidt's rise to Federal Chancellor of Germany and Giscard's to President of France transformed the meetings into political events of the highest rank. There were four members of this original club: the United States, Germany, France and the United Kingdom. At Schmidt's urging Japan was soon added to the round. Italy and Canada joined in 1975 and 1976 respectively. 'There was no question', Putnam and Bayne write, 'of heads of state and government meeting out of the public eye. When the leaders came together, this would arouse expectations of substantial achievements. Public opinion would look for progress where others had failed, since no higher level remained to which intractable problems could be referred.'[9] In the course of the 1970s and 1980s, media coverage increased those expectations. What leaders said during the summit and in their final declarations caused a worrying ambivalence: experts were sceptical about the usefulness of these meetings for an exchange of policy views, but the general public continued to look for significant results from them.

From the beginning Helmut Schmidt saw the annual summits as a way to build a framework of international consultation and policy collaboration among the Western allies. Although billed as 'economic' summits, the problems leaders from the G-7 nations discussed were seldom purely economic. Strategic and military questions, and various political issues on the world scene, often cut across their discussions of economic policy. The last German Chancellor to have served in the Second World War, Schmidt was acutely aware of the consequences that international political failure in the 1920s had had for his own country.[10]

Schmidt's pragmatic style was informed by a sense of the historical moment. Compared with his predecessor, Willy Brandt, Schmidt was less idealistic in his approach to SPD politics and his conception of Germany's place in the alliance, which were aimed more at improving the international atmosphere in support of German leadership. Schmidt was probably incapable of Brandt's *Kniefall* at a war memorial in Warsaw – a dramatic gesture that symbolized a different Germany, one opening to the East and more committed than its allies to detente with the Soviet Union. But he kept the initial momentum of Brandt's Ostpolitik going long after the US/Soviet relationship had cooled.

In the mid-1970s, Schmidt was at the height of his powers, and closely allied with French President Giscard d'Estaing. A Franco-German approach to most international issues could be amicably arranged. President Jimmy Carter proved an ineffective leader by contrast, and the British economy was so weak that neither Harold Wilson nor James Callaghan could take the initiative on the international level. Under Giscard's leadership the Rambouillet summit of 1975 reached agreement on a reform of exchange rates which gave rise to optimism that the instability in post-Bretton Woods monetary relations could be brought under control. Although these hopes were ultimately frustrated, the experience encouraged the Europeans, led by Schmidt and Giscard, to work for their own system of managed floating, as will be discussed in Chapter 5.[11]

The Americans wanted the emphasis elsewhere, however. With unemployment in the industrialized countries high, and the costs of energy still working their way through the economy, the Carter administration faced a raft of serious problems when it took office in 1977. The newly-elected President looked to America's allies with current-account surpluses, Germany and Japan, to take up the slack in the world economy.

From 1977 onwards, the Germans came under American and British pressure to stimulate their domestic economy and act as the 'locomotive' of Western economic recovery. They resisted from the start with arguments from the Bundesbank arsenal: domestic growth, projected at 4.5–5.5%, was high enough, and further stimulus would undermine the country's monetary stability. But despite this resistance, the Germans were beginning to shift their position. More pressure came in 1978 from within the European Community, and when Giscard and Schmidt announced their plan in April 1978 for a 'zone of monetary stability in Europe', many observers thought they saw a trade-off: the Germans would give their domestic economy more stimulus in exchange for greater monetary discipline elsewhere via the new EMS link to the mark.[12]

At the economic summit that summer in Bonn, Schmidt went into reverse on Germany's fiscal policy. This meeting was the high point of Schmidt's grand strategy. He wanted to link European interest in security and monetary stability with American foreign policy goals through the creation of new international institutions, primarily the European Monetary System. More exchange-rate stability in the Community would benefit German exports, and Schmidt's policy foresaw a more active role for the European Fund in covering national deficits. He hoped to reach agreement with Germany's partners on social policies that would reduce unemployment and guard against protective legislation. Stimulation of West German industry was promised by Schmidt in return.[13]

According to one analysis, Schmidt had already begun to shift position by autumn 1977 and was using the summit as a lever against domestic opponents of fiscal stimulus. The last of his converts to the new German policy was the Bundesbank. It temporarily surrendered one of the crucial elements of its own standard – no deficit financing and a balanced budget – and agreed to produce an estimate of how large a deficit would be supportable.[14] Schmidt's government considered something like 1% of GNP, or 12 billion marks, to be appropriate, and the Bank was persuaded by factors in the international economic environment to go along with the Chancellor's policy of fiscal stimulus. In the Bank's internal debate, the Keynesians won against the monetarists.

Germany's time as the 'locomotive' of the Western economies was short-lived, however. As discussed in Chapter 3, a combination of international and domestic political factors weakened the initially strong support for Schmidt's policy of fiscal stimulus at the Bonn summit, finally making it insupportable. From 1981 to 1985 the Bundesbank could successfully pursue a line of 'insular monetarism'.

Monetary policy under Plaza and Louvre: 1985 and after

By the second Bonn summit in 1985 America's problems had come to dominate the world's economic agenda. Its trade and budget deficits, coupled with the overvalued dollar, put pressure on the West European and Japanese economies. During its first term in office, the Reagan administration played down both, emphasizing the dramatic recovery in the US economy. From early 1985 onwards, however, the domestic debate in America began to shift. Treasury Secretary James Baker shared the concern of the Chairman of the Federal Reserve Board, Paul Volcker, over the worsening twin deficits.

These discussions led to the revival of the notion of international policy coordination – a shift away from the Reagan administration's previous view that economic policy was essentially a domestic matter. They also enhanced the role of finance ministers in international economic policy-making. Under James Baker's leadership, discussions got under way aimed at reducing the US deficit in exchange for stimulus in the economies of Japan and West Germany. Secretary of State George Shultz urged the Japanese to liberalize their capital markets, while Baker expressed his hope that 'the slack in the United States would be picked up by Europe and Japan'.[15] Trying to fight off domestic pressures for protectionist legislation and to keep the American economy out of recession, Baker urged his colleagues among the G-7 to take a dose of the American medicine: tax cuts to stimulate supply-led growth, and low interest rates to boost investment.

There was a taste of international coordination in late January 1985, when the G-5 Finance Ministers announced that 'the dollar was grossly overvalued and that this warranted concerted action'. In March and April the Bundesbank led central bank intervention to lower the dollar.[16]

The second Bonn summit in 1985 did little to further policy coordination of economic issues, and that failure led to Baker's initiative for a meeting of G-5 Finance Ministers at the Plaza Hotel in New York that September. When they came together that autumn after extensive bilateral consultations, the ministers could present a unified front on trade and the dollar. An 'orderly appreciation' of other currencies was called for, leading to a 4% devaluation of the US currency in one day. The following day President Reagan announced an aggressive trade strategy to counter allegedly unfair practices by America's trading partners. Success at the Plaza and the President's statement were enough to reduce protectionist sentiment in Congress and allow him to veto a bill limiting textile imports without fear of being overridden.

While the agreement announced at the Plaza fell short of Baker's wishes, it signalled an American commitment to policy coordination, abandoning the laissez-faire attitude of the United States towards exchange rates. When Congress passed the Gramm-Rudmann-Hollings Bill in December 1986, requiring a reduction of the deficit to zero by 1991, things seemed to be in place for further progress towards constructing a stable international monetary system. The Americans considered that they had kept their part of the bargain to get the deficit down and take over active management of the dollar.

These agreements were an implicit challenge to the Bundesbank paradigm. Exchange-rate policy traditionally belonged to the federal government, but if Plaza and Louvre were to be effective the Bundesbank would have to fund potentially large exchange-rate interventions. Policy-makers in the central bank thought the end of Bretton Woods had limited the internal-external balance problem. Now it was coming back step by step through less formal arrangements.

Inflation and the domestic economy in Germany: the paradigm in practice

By 1986 the terms of the discussion were clear: the Germans and Japanese wanted the Americans to apply more fiscal discipline to get their budget deficit and trade balance back in order; the Americans wanted Germany and Japan to stimulate demand in their own economies by cutting taxes and lowering interest rates. The Germans were more reluctant than the Japanese to follow the American lead after Plaza.[17] There were several reasons for their hard line on reflation and their resistance throughout 1986–7 to giving more leadership in the international economy. Some were short-term, such as the coming general election in January 1987, but all the German arguments referred to the basic position of the Bundesbank: there was no such thing as growth with inflation; rather, an inflation-free economy was the prerequisite for growth. In the two years between the Plaza agreement and the stock market crash of October 1987 this remained the Bundesbank position and it was supported by the German government.

Another factor was the Bundesbank's success against inflation during 1986–7. Although its March 1985 Report cautioned that inflationary pressures were building up, the Bundesbank could look back at the end of 1985 with considerable satisfaction. Writing for the conservative newspaper *Welt am Sonntag*, President Pöhl was optimistic that the three-year period of growth in the Federal Republic would continue into 1986: 'The level of monetary stability we have achieved at present is the most important foundation for continuous upturn. Every citizen, not least employees and pensioners, profits from stable prices.' The 'economic ecology' of recovery was right, Pöhl asserted: stable prices, a solid fiscal policy, moderate wage agreements. All this allowed a public policy in the Federal Republic which resulted in low interest rates, and the Bundesbank would continue to permit enough growth in the supply of money during 1986 to keep the recovery going.[18]

The drastic fall in energy prices and the equally dramatic devaluation of the dollar against the mark had a positive effect on prices in the Federal Republic. Import costs were on average 19% lower in 1986 than in 1985, largely as a result of the decline in oil prices. Crude oil was 60% cheaper in marks; petrol and heating oil were 55% cheaper. During 1985 the rate of inflation in Germany fell from 2.5% to a little less than 2%, but unemployment remained relatively high, at 8.1%. In the United States unemployment was 7% and inflation 3.5%. The discount rate in the United States averaged 8% and in Germany 4.5%. With growth in the Federal Republic at 3.5%, Pöhl had every reason to be cheerful about future prospects. In fact, during 1986 inflation went below 1% and kept falling, until by May of that year a slight disinflation had begun.

Still, not everybody in Germany agreed with Pöhl's assessment of German prospects for 1986. Whatever the official figures say, what counts for the voter is what he or she notices, and the half per cent fall in the price level by the end of 1985 was hardly dramatic. During the autumn, the Allensbach Institute for Public Opinion Research surveyed Germans on their perceptions of the economic situation, with results that must have disappointed the 'guardians of the currency' in Frankfurt. Only 40% noticed any success in the battle against inflation; the rest either could see no change or had no opinion. This seemed to indicate a psychological shift: memories of the great inflation of 1923 were fading, and the 'creeping inflation' of the early 1970s had produced a different public reaction. 'What seems painful at the moment and dampens pleasure over stability', the *Frankfurter Allgemeine Zeitung* commented, 'are the withdrawal symptoms that appear with an anti-inflation cure. Salaries and wages rise more slowly, overtime disappears. People talk about these things, naturally, but less about the fact that prices are rising more slowly and so what they have is worth more.'[19]

As memories of Germany's inflations in 1923 and after the Second World War receded, fear of unemployment became more concrete. By the mid-1980s it seemed to have displaced inflation *Angst*, and this fact did not go unnoticed by the political parties. While the Social Democrats continued to press for more state action to stimulate growth and create or save jobs, the governing coalition and its conservative supporters in the media resisted any measures that might reverse the beginnings of success over inflation. The cost of living rose by only 1.8% – a rate of increase in Germany not seen since the 1960s – and the prospect of a 'zero in front of the comma' was in sight. Bavarian Minister-President Franz Josef Strauss asserted that (contrary to the perceptions of the population) 'increases in wages are now getting through to the consumer and not being eaten up by inflation. Savings will hold their value, and won't melt away like spring snow in the sun.'[20]

The terms of debate in the clash between Helmut Schmidt and the Bundesbank from the early part of the decade continued to shape public opinion about inflation and growth at the end of 1985. The Christian Democrat coalition's 'resolute will for stability' was contrasted with the SPD/FDP coalition's calculation of 5% inflation rates. Although such party-political exchanges surprise no one, they are a key to deciphering the way domestic rhetoric plays into Germany's international economic policy through the 'inflation or growth' dilemma. At the beginning of the period of low to nil inflation, the example of Schmidt's government tolerating a relatively high inflation rate to expand the economy still shaped the domestic argument. During 1986–7 it was a constant reference point in the US-German dispute over interest rates and growth. If that was allowed to happen again, Bundesbank policy-makers argued, Germany would be back in the same position as in 1982: high inflation, high unemployment and a budget deficit.

The Bundesbank's exposed flank: 1986
In the early 1970s opponents and proponents of fixed exchange rates

had agreed on one thing: the transition to a system of floating currencies would make stabilization of the domestic economy easier.[21] Free of external obligations, central bank money management would become more flexible and could be better targeted. Policy-makers at the Bundesbank who had seen their efforts to control domestic inflation undermined by German obligations under Bretton Woods during 1960–1 and 1968–73 greeted the end of fixed exchange rates with relief, and their removal seemed at first to bring 'external factors under substantially better control'.[22]

By the end of 1986 the Bundesbank's autonomy had expanded little, if at all, and policy-makers there felt themselves increasingly trapped by international constraints. The outstanding feature of that year was the challenge of 'powerful external adjustment constraints'. These brought back the old problems of distortions in Germany's exports that caused speculative flows of foreign capital into the Federal Republic such as those experienced in 1973 and 1978. This then placed 'strict limits on the Bundesbank's monetary means to control powerful increases in the supply of money', with the consequence that 'for the first time since 1978, monetary goals were substantially exceeded'.[23] In response, the Bundesbank pursued a monetary policy that at first cautiously, then consistently, accommodated expansion of the money supply. The markets began 1986 with relatively low interest rates and the Bundesbank followed suit by reducing the discount rate from 4% to 3% in March. The Lombard rate stayed at 5%. Throughout the year the mark was under powerful pressure for revaluation.

The weaker position of the mark in the EMS, especially against the French franc, induced a new international capital flow in April, this time out of the mark. The banks' reduction in liquidity was met by 'exceptionally high' transfers of federal funds into the money supply, which the Bundesbank facilitated through an increased transfer of its profits to the federal government. The Bundesbank also increased the liquidity available to the banks via the bond market. At the same time new minimum reserve rules came into effect, releasing 7 billion marks to the banks.[24] The combination of reduced minimum reserves and the release of federal funds into the money markets meant that the banks had some 17 billion marks more at their disposal in 1986. As pressure for revaluation of the mark resumed in mid-year, the Bundesbank tried to accommodate it by increased liquidity, but its use of bonds fell to a relative low of 18 billion marks.

These problems in the monetary sector caused a 3% drop in West German exports during 1986, but the country's economy still grew by 2% in real terms. Output in manufacturing industry slowed down in 1986, but production of automobiles (a sector particularly sensitive to foreign demand) actually increased by 4% over the year. There was a powerful increase in building trades activity (4%) and in the service industries (3%), led by credit and insurance industries. More people were employed in 1986, causing the first fall in unemployment since the early 1980s. Overall investment was up by 6%, although this trend had begun to taper off by early 1987. Germans saved as much in 1986 as in 1985 (13%) but they also consumed more and reduced their indebtedness (the rate of new credit for private households fell by 20% in 1986). As prices in the Federal Republic continued to fall, the real standard of living rose and real incomes were up by 4%.

Summing up the general trends in Germany's domestic economy, the Bank's pointed analysis of domestic growth aimed at least as much at international as at domestic targets. In a version of the old 'locomotive strategy', the Americans had pressed West Germany during 1986 to stimulate its economy. The Bundesbank view of sustained domestic growth despite adverse external circumstances was a tacit rebuff to Baker and the US Treasury: domestic consumption in 1986 was able to compensate for the fall in Germany's exports. Its surplus, the Bank argued in its Annual Report, was exaggerated by

the fall in oil prices and powerful devaluation of the US dollar ... Just for energy alone, the Federal Republic has to pay nearly 40 billion marks less, or about half, what it paid in the year before... It is obvious that falls of this kind cannot be quickly compensated through contrary movements in trade with foreign countries... Dislocations are the result of variations in the speed of adjustment in prices and volumes in foreign trade.[25]

If the Bundesbank felt itself under increased international pressure during 1986, the following year brought a double dose of factors that plagued its stability paradigm.

The Bundesbank's exposed flank: 1987

Two international factors overshadowed 1987: the collapse of equity prices in October and the further destabilization of the dollar on world currency markets. Each provided new evidence of the Bundesbank's reduced autonomy, but the German economy as a whole weathered these shocks remarkably well. Growth was below 1986 at 1.7%. In 1987, as in 1986, domestic demand set the pace, growing at 3%; the Bundesbank remarked (no doubt with an eye on American critics of its sluggish economy) that this was 'a rate thoroughly respectable by international standards', and argued that:

> Since the second half of 1985, when foreign demand began to decline, households' consumption spending has increasingly become the major counterbalance. Private consumption stabilized the domestic economy and supported the external adjustment process, for the growing consumer demand was to a great extent focused on imports of goods and services... In real terms, private consumption rose by 3%.[26]

This was the strongest rate of increase since the late 1970s, and affected practically all sectors of the economy, including those which normally lag behind income growth. Against the pattern of increasing inflation during 1988–9, the Bundesbank's view of wage agreements in 1987 is particularly interesting. Largely as a result of trade union demands for a reduced working week (the 35-hour campaign), German employers signed a number of pay agreements that contained reductions in working hours and phased pay increases for the period up to and including 1989. Such agreements, the Bank commented, 'show the confidence management and labour have in price stability ... Such trust was warranted for 1987, is warranted for 1988 and naturally still has to be warranted for the period even further ahead.'[27]

In 1987 stability was imported again through falling costs for raw materials and energy generated by devaluation of the dollar against the mark and by OPEC's failure to sustain its initially higher prices for oil. With the cost of imported goods 6% less in 1987 than in the previous year, largely through an appreciating mark, the German economy had a comfortable buffer for its domestic price index.

Inflation, at somewhat less than 1%, was up on 1986 but still not a cause for alarm in the Bundesbank. In fact in its 1987 Report the Bank took pride in German success at keeping price increases well below those in its trading partners: 3% in both the US and the other EC countries.

The darker side of the German economy in 1986–7 was a stubbornly high unemployment rate and marked differences between the northern and southern Länder. The unemployment problem appeared in the Bundesbank's official publications as a marginal issue: for skilled males, prepared to work full-time and follow job opportunities, its analysis implied, there was no unemployment problem. The unemployed were women, part-time workers, school-leavers and above all those without skills for the marketplace. Moreover, Baden-Württemberg, Bavaria and Hesse all reported lower unemployment levels than the northern Länder, and in the south employment and economic prospects in general were much brighter.[28]

Some of that difference can be accounted for in terms of the relative age of each region's industrial base. Northern Germany, like northern England, was the area of the old heavy industries of shipbuilding and steel. The Ruhr, with its coal mines and steelworks, is much like northeast England and Scotland. Although they kept going in the world markets longer than British industries (partly through the German institution of the *Kohlenpfennig*, or coal tax, to spread the costs of unproductive but socially necessary industries over the whole nation), these areas of heavy industry in Germany were coming under increasing pressure from cheaper manufacturers. One reason for decreased investment in machinery and equipment in relation to profits and the favourable interest-rate climate in 1987, the Bundesbank noted, was the 'uncertainty as to future trends in this area and the ongoing structural crisis in some particularly capital-intensive sectors (mining, steel production, shipbuilding) as industry has to shoulder the main burden of the external adjustment process'.[29]

Giving way: the domestic costs of international cooperation

The coordination of monetary efforts to pump liquidity into the world banking system, cut interest rates and stabilize exchange rates after the crash of 1987 was a remarkable example of international coordination. The most important institutional elements in that effort had been created over the preceding decade: the meetings of the G-7 nations had established consultation practices that could be turned into coordination mechanisms in a crisis.

But these mechanisms, so effective in the 1987 crisis, also channelled international pressure onto the Bundesbank. This reached an intensity in 1986 and 1987 that directly undermined its paradigm approach to monetary sovereignty in Germany. In 1986, the Bank had failed to stay within its 'corridor' of 3–5% growth in the money supply. Even during the first quarter of that year, the increase was faster than the corridor allowed. During the first months of 1986 pressure for a realignment in the EMS produced renewed foreign capital inflows – a classic example of the exposed flank problem – and led to a further growth in the money supply. By mid-1986 these pressures had eased, so that the Bundesbank could hope to get back into the corridor over the remaining months of the year. But instead the money supply increased dramatically, at one point reaching 9%. By the end of 1986, it had grown by 7.7% – over 2% above the top of the corridor.

Throughout this period, the Bundesbank tolerated such increases. Explaining its policy, the Bank pointed specifically to the constraints of the international monetary system:

The powerful revaluation of the D-Mark particularly against the US dollar – at times covered by D-Mark interventions – and the tendency towards weakness of the currencies of some important partners in the EMS restricted the Bundesbank's room for manoeuvre. An attempt to limit monetary expansion through interest-rate and liquidity policy would presumably have sharpened the revaluation tendency of the D-Mark. In addition the expansionary monetary policy that resulted had the effect of producing a desired shift from imports to domestic goods and thus contributed to the reduction of asymmetries in the international economy.[30]

Much the same constellation faced the Bundesbank in 1987: in the face of a money supply that was growing faster than planned, international factors constrained its use of traditional instruments of monetary control. Now this provoked a tone of mounting anxiety in the Bundesbank. It had continued its 'efforts to prevent monetary expansion from getting completely out of hand in the longer run, although 1987 saw another overshooting of the target corridor set for growth of the central bank money stock'. In the Bundesbank paradigm, domestic issues take priority over international monetary issues – or at least they are meant to do so. But 1987 presented the Bank with the bill, as one official remarked, for Germany's international engagements. Its Annual Report sounds a melancholy note: 'The strong impact of external constraints on the stance of monetary policy . . . stood in the way of a domestic orientation.'[31]

The policy struggle going on in the Central Bank Council focused at the theoretical level on the familiar issue of general economic goals versus monetary stability. The crucial years from 1985 to 1987 began with the apparent triumph of Claus Köhler's 'generalist' strategy and closed with the doubts raised by Helmut Schlesinger and others. Analysing its policy for 1985, the Bundesbank referred to 'continuity and flexibility in monetary policy'. Growth in the supply of money through 1985 had been reduced by about 1% in comparison to 1984 (from 4–6% to 3–5%), a fact that did not mean tighter money for the economy, the Bundesbank noted, but merely 'reflected the monetary stability of the previous year'. As a starting-point the Bundesbank took one of Köhler's theoretical maxims, orienting its money supply goal on Germany's economic potential for 1985: the expected increase in productivity in relation to current prices. In 1982 and 1983 the money supply had been similarly increased by reference to a 'potential orientation'.[32]

For 1985 and 1986 this strategy seemed to have worked – at least in terms of the Bundesbank's primary concern, stability of the currency. West Germany began the longest period of declining prices and increased living standards since the 1950s. But the Central Bank Council was split even then over the effects of Köhler's theory, and as the Bank overshot its targets during 1986 and 1987 there was increasing opposition to it. 'We knew this growth in the money supply had to come out somewhere,' one Bundesbank official argued, in a conversation with the author, 'but there was little – given the massive international pressure on the Bundesbank during 1986 – we could do to get it back under control.' Pressure came from two sources: the USA (and its large budget imbalances) and the EMS. That view echoes the Bank's public analysis of the money supply in 1987. Increased liquidity from foreign-exchange interventions to support the dollar and keep the EMS bands solid amounted to 22 billion marks. By January 1988, as the Bundesbank Annual Report of 1987 makes clear, it had basically lost control of the money markets. Use of its open-market instrument, short-term securities, reached the lowest level in three years (16.4 billion marks). By February 1988 the Bundesbank began to offset liquidity growth by reducing the banks' refinancing facilities by 6 billion marks. Throughout this period (October 1987 to January 1988) the Bundesbank was severely constrained by international factors: 'the external situation prompted the Bundesbank to refrain from measures which – though they could not have guaranteed meeting the 1987 monetary target – might at least have better contained the overshooting'.[33]

The international pressures building up on the Bundesbank had a long background. The insistence that interest rates be lowered became 'absolutely massive' at the beginning of 1986. Bundesbank concerns about money supply targets, according to one official, were simply 'not accepted in the international context and [it] was under constant pressure to play the lead-rider role'. This international pressure, combined with the appearance of speculative capital flows from abroad, shaped Bundesbank policy discussions throughout the year. Although there were ample institutional forums for discussion of its concerns, Bundesbank policy-makers throughout 1986–7 felt themselves backed into a corner and 'simply isolated'. As inflation and the money supply figures began to get out of control towards the end of 1988 a sense of *Schadenfreude* among Bundesbank policy-makers made itself felt. For one faction, now possibly the most powerful in the Bundesbank, the experience of 1985–8 confirmed the central element of the Bundesbank paradigm: protect the currency at all costs.

But in the economic context of 1987, their options were few. Higher interest rates, the traditional instrument to deal with money supply, had obvious political disadvantages. They would have meant a sharp conflict with the United States plus even sharper devaluation of the US dollar, and would have unsettled the EMS. The result was an unusual curve on German money markets – short-term interest rates were at 2–3% while long-term rates stood at 6–7%. The Bundesbank believed this discrepancy could not be maintained and in 1986–7 interest rates began to come down. Under the friendly circumstances of very low to negative inflation, the Bundesbank began notching its rates down over half a year. For nineteen months they stayed firm – and the Bundesbank was criticized by both sides. In 1986–7, with real interest rates at 6%, the Bundesbank 'practically bought the whole foreign state indebtedness' and tried in that way to buy goodwill abroad. This policy was 'inefficient': 'we failed with the low interest-rates policy'. No government took the Bank's warnings of inflationary dangers seriously and expectations were raised unrealistically.

How could the Bank's policy in 1986–7 have been more efficient? Only through getting the money supply under control and through a strong mark, but one official remarked: 'we used a weak mark to put up interest rates'. A similar view on the relationship between interest rates and money supply has been expressed by Helmut Schlesinger, whose views represent the domestic faction on the CBC. They start with the first principle of the Bundesbank ethos: that a central bank's specific role in the modern economy is to protect the currency. Stable money is the precondition and basis for a functional market economy, and the Bank's means to assure monetary stability is control of the money supply. 'No other institution of government can do this.'[34] The Bundesbank should not peg interest rates, they argue, because this always produces a shortfall between stated goals and the results of high/low interest-rate policy. In the end 'easy money policy' always leads through inflation to higher interest rates. Money supply targets, by contrast, are more flexible, demonstrating the central bank's intention and thus decisively shaping the norms and structures of the economy. For the present the greatest challenge to its ability to control the money supply and ensure the domestic stability of the economy comes from the volatility of exchange rates and the ensuing flows of capital.

In the view of one top Bundesbank official, 'the shackles came back with the G-7': the international web of agreements, announcements, and attempts at coordination of monetary strategy and economic policy among the largest industrial nations have produced constraints not unlike those the Bundesbank chafed at under the old Bretton Woods arrangement. For a shifting faction on the Central Bank Council the issue is always the domestic economy and the Bundesbank's primary legal obligation to it: what effect does cooperation and working together have on domestic stability? In August 1987, that view prevailed at a crucial point when the Bundesbank wanted to put up rates for short-term securities repurchases.[35]

Looking back on the turbulence of 1987, the Bundesbank reported a surprising recovery in the world economy for the following year. This success resulted mostly from the cooperation of the industrialized countries, which 'through agreed monetary relaxation worked closely together to limit loss of trust in the economy and stabilize future expectations'.[36] Production demonstrated a remarkable insulation from disturbances on the financial markets. With real growth of 4%, industrial countries achieved their second-best year of growth in eighteen years and world trade expanded sharply by 9%.

Some familiar problems remained, however. Unemployment stayed relatively high; in the Bundesbank's view this was because of structural conditions unrelated to business cycle movements which monetary stimulation would not help (the implicit reference was to 1980–1). Rather, 'rigidities' on the labour market, such as worker immobility, lack of qualifications or inappropriate job expectations on the part of the unemployed were the true cause of unemployment. Imbalances in international trade remained and Britain joined the United States, in the Bundesbank's opinion, as a country with a worrying deficit.[37] Compared with the previous year, the US deficit had not caused such disruptions on the exchange markets. The Bank regarded the dollar, which was at or near the top of its Louvre band, as clearly too high. Just as its Annual Report for 1988 appeared, the US currency resumed its upward flight, accompanied by increases in the Bank's interest rates.[38] These movements in exchange and interest rates seemed part of the Bank's general worries over inflation. An overall price increase of 3.6% drew the Bank's attention and it warned that, while the increases might not be noticeable in individual countries, they spelled trouble over the medium term, especially as production was at near-capacity in the industrialized nations.

Conclusions

The crisis year 1987 was an exceptional case that reveals a pattern of policy-making in Germany's central bank, the main features of which are as follows:

(1) The international dimension of Bundesbank policy-making is long-standing and dates back to Bretton Woods, but the form

of conflicts over 'imported inflation' has changed under the regime of floating rates. From the early 1960s to the mid-1970s, the Bundesbank viewed inflation generated outside Germany as the main threat to monetary stability, and Bank officials believed their control over this factor would increase once they were released from mandatory intervention. Interdependence proved that expectation vain. Since the 1970s, economic relations have been 'internationalized' through autonomous capital movements and market expectations that are beyond the control of states to a greater degree than ever before.[39]

(2) As Germany emerges as the pre-eminent European economic power, international attention on the Bundesbank is generating new pressures on it. Defined essentially in terms of its domestic legislation, the Bank is a national institution increasingly subject to international demands. These force it to justify its decisions in terms which do not match its paradigm.

(3) Institutional changes in the past two decades are one aspect of these transformations; as the number of participants in international monetary policy-making decreases, the political power of those still involved increases. During a period of intensifying interdependence, the number of those who really matter in the international system has remained very small. The more exclusive circles of G-7 and G-3 leaders have supplanted the International Monetary Fund, which has more than 100 member countries. Within that framework the Deutschmark is now the world's second reserve and intervention currency. This has inevitably enhanced the power of the Bundesbank.

(4) The Bundesbank tends to balance domestic responsibilities against international pressures, consistently emphasizing the priority of the former. Its domestic and international policy choices in the years 1961, 1979–82 and 1985–7 are likely to remain the formative cases for its attitude in the future. International issues have greatly complicated the Bank's field of political action, and its rhetoric has to be seen in the context of its pragmatic responses to Germany's political interests and to pressure from its trade partners. Although it misjudged reactions to interest-rate policy immediately before the crash of 1987, the Bundesbank responded constructively to the emergency on the world's equity markets. While the Bundesbank standard remains the norm of monetary policy,

those events showed that the constitutive elements of its institutional identity can be modified or even suspended.

How does the Bundesbank's policy standard shape its approach to normal international demands? The Bank's management of the European Monetary System is the central case, and will be examined in the next chapter.

5

THE EUROPEAN MONETARY SYSTEM

If the international monetary system shows increasing signs that no single currency can play the dollar's old role, regional prospects in Europe look very different. Over the first decade of the European Monetary System, the mark played a crucial role in bringing down the inflation rates of Germany's EMS partners, creating the conditions for a more stable monetary regime in Europe. But in the next steps towards monetary union, the Bundesbank's position is facing a renewed challenge. How have its experiences as monetary anchor of the EMS been assimilated into the Bundesbank's outlook? Does its role constrain the Bank's policies? How do its policy-makers view economic and monetary trends in Europe on the eve of the single market and in the light of the 1989 Delors Committee Report on European Monetary Union?

EMS – the Bundesbank perspective ten years on
Many in the Community accept Walter Hallstein's argument that 'monetary policy is the keystone' to European integration.[1] Although European heads of government are now formally committed to monetary union, lack of consensus on how to achieve that goal indicates continuing differences of view over the distribution of institutional power in a political constitution for the Community.

Monetary union was first proposed in the Werner Report (1969).[2] In some ways ahead of its time politically, this report reflected the influence of the Bretton Woods system that was just then beginning to disintegrate. The 'snake in the tunnel', which ultimately (after French and British flirtations) involved a number of small countries in a Deutschmark zone, was the next step in European monetary integration. This was followed in 1979 by the agreement to form the European Monetary System, which was linked specifically to EC membership and included all EC states as members, although not everyone was a full member.[3] Its explicit intention was to create 'a zone of monetary stability' in Europe, as noted in Chapter 4. Its heart was the Exchange Rate Mechanism (ERM), a system of exchange-rate bands establishing relative values as fixed but flexible links between national currencies. Each currency could fluctuate within a margin of plus or minus 2.25% around its central rate, except for the wider band of the Italian lira. When a currency moved too close to the top or bottom of its band, the central banks of the EMS member countries were obliged to intervene, selling the stronger currency and buying the weaker one. Mutually agreed mechanisms for carrying out intervention, including the creation of a common fund to finance operations – the European Monetary Cooperation Fund (EMCF) – from which members could draw, were intended to coordinate and support the European central banks' activities in the markets.

Other aspects of the system implied more complex goals of sharing the burdens (and powers) of monetary stability and encouraging more equal relations of trade and investment in Europe. The ecu, created simultaneously, was intended as the intervention currency of the new system and as a symbol of the way forward towards European monetary union.[4] No other concrete steps were taken in 1979, and it was left to the markets to decide whether a role could be found for the ecu.

The Bundesbank initially opposed the European Monetary System.[5] The EMCF was a particular obstacle: the Bank feared that obligatory intervention and a joint financing mechanism would bring back the familiar problems of Bretton Woods. These would turn the EMS into an artificial exchange-rate system divorced from economic fundamentals, thus generating inflationary pressures in Germany. Concern over the implications of the EMS for the Bundesbank's autonomy in monetary policy led the Bank's officials to insist that the EMCF must not give automatic drawing rights to countries whose currency came under market pressure. After difficult negotiations between Helmut Schmidt and the central bank, including a threat by the Chancellor to amend the Bundesbank Law if the Bank did not agree to the EMS, a compromise was reached which allowed the Bank enough autonomous judgment in managing exchange rates to allay its fears about government encroachment on its independence.[6]

In its first year the EMS appeared to revive the 'exposed flank' problem (discussed in Chapter 4) in a specifically European guise, and the Bundesbank saw it as creating another external threat to the stability of the German currency. In the vital area of intervention, EMS theory and the reality of its management quickly parted ways. The 1979 agreement stipulated that currency-market intervention should take place in the currency of the intervening central bank. By the end of the first year, however, the mark had become the normal intervention currency of the EMS, taking on the role originally foreseen for the ecu. Looking back on the first year of the new monetary system, the European Commission's *Annual Economic Report, 1979/80* noted that for most of the first four months of its existence, the mark had been at or near the top of its EMS band. Its position reflected the persistent strength of the German economy and continued upward pressure on the mark from international sources.

In sheer volume terms, the dollar relationship remained pre-eminent. The Commission's report noted that most central bank interventions during 1979–80 were to control dollar movements and continued to take place in dollars. As the world economy went through the second oil price shock of 1979, the dollar dropped sharply. While there was little intervention by the US Federal Reserve, the dollar-mark relationship was the crucial parity in the first year of the EMS. In succeeding years dollar-mark strains remained an important source of pressure on the EMS. More direct, if minor, pressures on the EMS came from exclusively European tensions, such as the effect realignment might have on the Common Agricultural Policy.

The Bundesbank's initial reluctance to play an enlarged role in the international monetary system showed in its sharp official comments on the EMS. The first EMS realignment in September 1979 caused Bundesbank President Otmar Emminger to declare that it would not be in the interests of stable money in Germany for the mark to become a reserve currency. 'Under no circumstance', Emminger said then, 'should the Federal Republic become a dumping ground for the unloved dollar which would only expose it to imported infla-tion.'[7] The Bank's concerns at that time – the threat such a role posed to its power over the domestic-international interface in monetary affairs – continue to guide its policy today, even though, as we shall see below, Europe's monetary system developed quite differently from the Bundesbank's expectations.

After an initial phase of relative instability, with seven revalua-tions across the system in the four years from 1979 to 1983, the EMS settled down. During the next five-year period rates of exchange were adjusted only five times (see Table 1).

Table 1 EMS realignments: changes in bilateral central bank rates (%)

		German mark	Belgian franc	Danish krone	French franc	Irish punt	Italian lira	Dutch guilder
1979	24 Sept.	+2		−2.86				
	30 Nov.			−4.76				
1981	23 Mar.						−6	
	5 May	+5.5			−3		−3	+5.5
1982	22 Feb.		−8.5	−3				
	14 June	+4.25			−5.75		−2.75	+4.25
1983	21 Mar.	+5.5	+1.5	+2.5	−2.5	−3.5	−2.5	+3.5
1985	22 July	+2	+2	+2	+2	+2	−6	+2
1986	7 Apr.	+3	+1	+1	−3			+3
	4 Aug.					−8		
1987	12 Jan.	+3	+2					+2

Sources: Deutsche Bundesbank; J. Fels, *Intereconomics,* no. 5, 1987.

In the eleven EMS realignments so far, the mark has always appreciated, whereas the French franc has usually been devalued, resulting in a 37% loss in its original parity value against the mark. The franc devaluations had a substantial impact on national interest rates, the cost of imported goods and the imponderables of 'national prestige'. For this reason French politicians have tended to see exchange rates in a political context beyond the managerial con-siderations advanced by central bankers. From the French perspec-tive, the struggle over the EMS centres on the perceived hegemony of Bundesbank policy – a powerful position that subtly determines the shape of French national economic policy and blocks 'Europeanization' of the Community's economies.

From the Bundesbank's perspective, the EMS is a balancing act in which the Bundesbank standard is juggled with international and European responsibilities. Exchange-rate policy is sensitive because of the postulated link between money supply targets and inflation; systems such as the EMS (like Bretton Woods earlier) constrain the Bank's pursuit of the domestic stability goal. Though central banks are obliged to intervene when currencies hit the top or bottom of their bands, their intervention before that stage remains discretionary. Conflicts of judgment and interest over when to intervene shape the politics of EMS management and carry implications for the Bundesbank's strategy of controlling inflation.

The Bundesbank distinguishes between inflation as a medium-term monetary phenomenon and substantial changes in the

Table 2 Monetary targets and actual outcomes (%)

Year	Target: growth of central bank money stock or M_3*		Actual outcome (rounded figures)		Target achieved
	Q4 to Q4	annual average	Q4 to Q4	annual average	
1975	around 8	—	10	—	no
1976	—	8	—	9	no
1977	—	8	—	9	no
1978	—	8	—	11	no
1979	6–9	—	6	—	yes
1980	5–8	—	5	—	yes
1981	4–7	—	4	—	yes
1982	4–7	—	6	—	yes
1983	4–7	—	7	—	yes
1984	4–6	—	5	—	yes
1985	3–5	—	5	—	yes
1986	$3\frac{1}{2}$–$5\frac{1}{2}$	—	8	—	no
1987	3–6	—	8	—	no
1988	3–6	—	7	—	no
1989	around 5	—			

*From 1988: money supply M_3.
Sources: Deutsche Bundesbank; H. Sherman, *Tokyo Club Papers*, no. 3, 1990.

economic structure which produce long-term inflationary results. Since 1979 it has set a 'corridor' for growth in the money supply, not a fixed percentage for each year, which it has not always been able to maintain, as Table 2 shows. The money supply target is composed of four variables: projected growth of productive potential; desirable change in capacity utilization; the 'unavoidable' rate of inflation; and expected changes in money velocity.[8] In that equation, inflation is 'a normative item' that has usually been set at one-half to one per cent below the projected rate.[9] The Bundesbank stability norm thus allows for some expansion of the money supply, but increases or decreases in money supply that do not reflect *expected* production and price variables are resisted vigorously. The most important source of such distortions, in the Bundesbank's view, are exchange-rate operations related to the market values of EMS currencies and the dollar.

Managing the system: Germany's Bretton Woods

Formal alignment of EMS currencies is a political decision taken by the European finance ministers and governments. The Bundesbank advises the German government in this process, but does not decide the timing or rates of realignment.[10] Its power in the present monetary system is exercised between realignments in the strategy and tactics of intervention.

The bands established at each revaluation determine the lines of obligatory intervention. Only when two currencies are at the extremities of their relative values are the two central banks required to intervene to protect the agreed cross-rates. The signal for such intervention is normally given when a weak currency drops to the bottom of its band value. Intervention follows the request of the central bank whose currency is being used. Because the mark is the leading intervention currency of the EMS, such conventions enhance the Bundesbank's power in Europe. To date it has been used to achieve wider acceptance of the norms of the Bundesbank standard: sound money and a realistic view of monetary and economic policy.

Intervention – procedures and power

The practice of EMS intervention directly links domestic goals and international policy – and thus defines the European political context of the Bundesbank's pursuit of its stability norm.

As a side-effect of securing exchange-rate targets, intervention changes the domestic money supply. Thus a devaluing country buys up its currency in exchange for foreign reserves (its own, borrowed or swapped). This reduces liquidity in that country, forcing up domestic interest rates, tightening monetary policy and reducing inflation. The effects for the economy of the appreciating country are the reverse. Appreciation creates more purchasing power, which is used to accumulate foreign exchange, thus increasing money supply in the medium term and hence inflation.[11] Theoretically, then, the exchange values of two (or more) currencies represent the ratio of their money stocks. If the price of currencies is fixed (as it is under international mechanisms such as the ERM), then the stocks will have to be adjusted to maintain the ratio. That holds true for each of the three types of EMS intervention: (1) *marginal intervention* and (2) *intramarginal interventions* (both in EMS currencies); and (3) *intramarginal intervention in US dollars*.[12]

While the technique of EMS interventions involves relatively simple operations, their practice is another story in political terms. Central banks may try to offset changes in domestic liquidity brought about by foreign exchange-market interventions through open-market activities (buying and selling government bonds). The increases or decreases in liquidity are thus 'sterilized', and consequently the exchange rate has to change in the medium term.

Exchange-rate policy forces a question of judgment on governments: is the attack on its currency motivated by short-term interests that will fade, or do fluctuations in exchange rates reflect long-term problems in the domestic economy? If a government believes its domestic policy has been correctly set, or if its policies give preference to other domestic goals, it may prefer to absorb short-term fluctuations in exchange rates. But the power to pursue that course is a function of the country's monetary (and ultimately its economic) position: it is easier for appreciating countries to sterilize foreign-exchange intervention and maintain their preferred domestic policy course because they can sell the domestic currency for a period and sterilize with comfort. Depreciators, on the other hand, run out of reserves and credit-worthiness quickly. From their perspective, asymmetry is the rule. In a system such as the EMS depreciating countries have less power to pursue domestic policy goals and manage their international obligations advantageously than appreciators do.

Power in the European Monetary System can be understood, then, as a function of the intervention capacity of ERM member central banks. Ability to affect exchange rates depends on their holdings of the intervention currency. Because nearly all interventions are carried out in marks, this means effectively that a central bank's power within the EMS is a measure of its Deutschmark strength.

The asymmetry debate focuses on the relative imbalance of intervention costs, particularly between France and Germany. Their positions as depreciator and appreciator define each country's EMS politics, and their circumstances since the start of the system illustrate the gap between its theory and practice. The domestic costs of its EMS interventions throughout the 1980s were carried by the French economy. It saw the EMS as an imbalanced or asymmetrical system in which Deutschmark strength enforced domestic anti-inflationary policies favoured by the Bundesbank. While that eventually led to reduced French inflation rates, France joined the hard-currency countries at the cost of relative national autonomy. Its demands for increased 'symmetry' aim at regaining some of that freedom of decision. Institutionalizing intramarginal interventions and strengthening automatic funding mechanisms such as the EMCF would help insulate a depreciating country's domestic economy from exchange-rate pressures – and simultaneously increase the exchange-rate effects on the appreciating country. The more automatic intervention is, the more difficult it is for an appreciating currency to control the use of its reserves. The EMS and the ecu-led divergence indicator were intended to reduce asymmetry, a goal the Bundesbank feared from the beginning. For the Bundesbank, symmetry spelled inflation.

The story of the EMS, however, developed along quite a different line. Far from bending its policies to those goals, the Bank was able to force asymmetry – and thus the stable money policies favoured by the Germans – on other members of the ERM despite the expressed objectives of the European Monetary System. As long as the mark remains the 'anchor currency' of the EMS, the Bundesbank can both pursue its primary domestic goal – a stable currency – and agree to international cooperation, because its power within the system achieves an adequate coordination of domestic and European goals. But proposals to increase automatic interventions threaten that harmony, raising the question of how far the power of a major appreciating country to meet domestic objectives would be reduced by such rules.

Day-to-day EMS management: the Bundesbank view
Once the request for intervention is agreed to by the central bank of the intervention currency, the mechanics of market intervention take place with a view to an orchestrated effect. Four times daily all the major central banks involved in the currency markets confer on exchange-rate developments. In Europe this goes on all day, with scheduled telephone conferences at 9.30, 11.30, 14.30 and 16.00. The US Federal Reserve begins to participate at 10.30 EST (16.30 Continental time). The Bank of Japan watches markets in the Far East overnight and confers as necessary with its European and American partners.

The International Division of the Bundesbank is the locus of consultation with other central banks and carries out German interventions in the market, focusing on three main currency relations: the dollar, the yen and EMS currencies. Other currencies being actively traded on the exchange markets may also be watched. A confidential activity sheet produced at the end of each day and circulated in-house gives an overview of central bank activity for the day. Graphs charting the movement of EMS currencies within their bands over a period of weeks are also produced by the International Division. These documents are regularly consulted in the fortnightly meetings of the CBC, which draws on them and their analysis in setting its policy towards voluntary interventions within the bands, the so-called 'intramarginal interventions' that are an increasingly prominent feature of the Bank's international activity.

The Bundesbank views its management of the German currency on the international markets as 'more an art than a science'. The more active role of the central banks after Bretton Woods has not shaken its outlook on the relation between exchange rates and the fundamentals of monetary and economic policy. The general lesson of 1980–81 and 1983, one Bundesbank official remarked in a conversation with the author, was that 'foreign-exchange interventions only have a lasting effect when supplemented by monetary policy. You have to have money growth under control and the interest rates realistically in line with your major partners' overall economic position before they will do any real good.' In other words, a combination of intervention and monetary policy are needed. This is the 'solid base' Bundesbank officials like to talk about when the subject of exchange-rate stability comes up.

Contrary to the Bundesbank's initial fears, the EMS has proved manageable within its anti-inflationary framework, and the Bank is generally satisfied with its working.[13] Although the Bank's rhetoric often implies a beleaguered position in the EMS, Germany's economic power laid the foundations of Bundesbank *Realpolitik*: its role as monetary anchor of the EMS broke the formal requirements of symmetry and allowed the system to be run on Bundesbank rules. But the ERM challenges the dominant 'economist' view in the Bundesbank of monetary development in Europe. Its political implications are the source of a more profound worry among policy-makers in Frankfurt. While the EMS can be made to work on their terms, it channels political pressures onto the Bank which are proving difficult to manage in the context of European economic unification, and could ultimately undermine the Bundesbank's definition as an independent central bank. The story of two realign-ments illustrates that point.

From crisis management to institutional change: a tale of two realign-ments

The last two EMS realignments (shown in Table 1 above) occurred in April 1986 and January 1987. During that period many of the underlying political tensions in the system generated by the Bundesbank standard surfaced, and acrimonious Franco-German exchanges marked the second event. These realignments added momentum to proposals for institutional reform that took shape in an agreement made by finance ministers in the Danish town of Nyborg in September 1987 and in the Delors Committee's Report on Monetary Union.

The 1986 and 1987 realignments occurred despite a marked convergence of inflation rates among European countries. While no other country achieved Germany's negative inflation rate in 1986, all its major partners showed lower rates of increase for the year. The average inflation rate for the whole of the Community was down to

4.4%; consumer prices in the Federal Republic's ERM partner countries stood at 3.5%, while for EC members outside the ERM inflation averaged 6.4% (see Tables 3 and 4). There remained, however, enough of an inflation differential between Germany and the others to generate market expectations of a mark revaluation. Comparative domestic factors in prices and production encouraged these expectations, and a weak dollar increased demand for the mark.

Table 3 Consumer prices in the EC 1981–6

Country/ group of countries	1981	1982	1983	1984	1985	1986[1]
			% change against previous year			
FRG	6.3	5.3	3.3	2.4	2.2	−0.2
ERM participants:[2]	**13.6**	**12.3**	**10.1**	**7.8**	**6.3**	**3.3**
France	13.4	11.8	9.6	7.4	5.8	2.7
Italy	17.9	16.5	14.7	10.8	9.2	5.9
Netherlands	6.7	5.9	2.8	3.3	2.3	0.2
Belgium	7.6	8.7	7.7	6.3	4.9	1.3
Denmark	11.7	10.1	6.9	6.3	4.7	3.6
Ireland	20.5	17.1	10.5	8.6	5.4	3.9
Luxembourg	8.1	9.4	8.7	4.6	4.1	0.3
Other EC partners[2]	**13.6**	**11.3**	**8.2**	**8.3**	**8.0**	**6.2**
UK	11.9	8.6	4.6	5.0	6.1	3.4
Spain[3]	14.6	14.4	12.2	11.3	8.8	8.8
Greece	24.5	21.0	20.2	18.5	19.3	23.0
Portugal[3]	20.0	22.4	25.5	29.3	19.3	11.7
All EC members[2]	**13.6**	**11.9**	**9.4**	**8.0**	**6.9**	**4.4**
Price increases in other countries relative to the FRG (%)						
ERM participants	6.9	6.6	6.6	5.3	4.0	3.5
Other EC partners	6.9	5.7	4.7	5.8	5.7	6.4
All EC members	6.9	6.3	5.9	5.5	4.6	4.6

Notes: [1] Provisional.
[2] Including private consumer expenditure 1981–3.
[3] Member since beginning of 1986.
Sources: FRG national statistics; OECD.

By late spring, those pressures forced a realignment of the system at the request of the French government. The mark and the Dutch guilder were revalued by 3%, the Belgian and Luxembourg franc

Table 4 Inflation rates—ERM and non-ERM countries

	Arithmetic average (in %)		Standard deviation	
	ERM[1]	Non-ERM[2]	ERM[1]	Non-ERM[2]
1974	13.5	12.6	3.9	4.9
1975	12.6	11.6	4.6	5.1
1976	10.8	8.5	4.5	4.0
1977	9.8	8.2	4.2	4.0
1978	7.2	6.4	3.2	2.9
Average 1974–78	**10.7**	**9.5**	**3.8**	**4.2**
1979	8.7	7.1	4.2	3.6
1980	12.0	10.6	5.7	4.2
1981	12.0	9.8	5.2	3.1
1982	10.8	7.4	4.3	2.8
1983	7.9	4.9	3.9	2.4
1984	6.4	4.9	2.7	1.7
1985	4.9	4.4	2.2	1.7
Average 1979–85	**8.9**	**7.0**	**3.9**	**2.8**

Notes: [1] Countries participating in the ERM (Belgium, Denmark, France, Germany, Ireland, Italy, Netherlands).
[2] Austria, Canada, Japan, Sweden, Switzerland, United Kingdom, United States.
Sources: IMF: *International Financial Statistics, Yearbook 1986;* J. Fels, *Intereconomics,* no. 5, 1987.

and the Danish krone by 1%, and the French franc was devalued by 3%. The mark emerged from the realignment in a relatively weak position against the French franc. Following the normal pattern of EMS realignments, the values of 'weak' and 'strong' currencies were reversed so that, for example, the mark's value against the French franc fell to the bottom of its band.

Commenting on the period following the April realignment, the Bundesbank noted there had been sizeable 'obligatory purchases of marks, especially by the Banque de France'. Other measures were also taken to stabilize the system. German interest rates had been reduced in January 1986 and the realignment, combined with overall financial convergence, made room for interest-rate reductions elsewhere.

The effect on German money stock was tolerable for the Bundesbank. Insofar as the purchases of marks went through the Bundesbank, they reduced the reserves of domestic German banks, but overall liquidity in the Bundesbank system increased. The Bank compensated for this by increasing its scheduled payment to the German government on 10 April from DM 5 billion (in 1985) to DM 8 billion. It also concluded a securities repurchase agreement with German banks on 16 April. Some of the central bank purchases of marks were also converted into dollars at the Bundesbank, decreasing its net external holdings of the American currency.

That realignment did not stabilize the system, however, and from mid-1986 the European central banks were again engaged in supporting purchases to shore it up. In part this was due to the fall in the dollar following the Plaza meeting of finance ministers. The mark's initial weakness was short-lived, and from June 1986 its value against the dollar began to increase. Although, according to the Bundesbank, this 'quasi-automatically' increased the value of other EMS currencies too, these lagged behind the mark's increase and set up new tensions in the system. In August the Irish punt was devalued. Towards the end of the year tensions in the system increased again, largely provoked by the continuing fall of the dollar. Demand for the mark and the Dutch guilder increased, and other EMS currencies weakened.

This second period of tension saw massive intramarginal interventions to stabilize the bands. The French franc, Irish punt and Danish krone all fell beneath their obligatory intervention points before the end of the year. In the week preceding the realignment on 12 January 1987, 16 billion marks were spent in intramarginal interventions to support weak currencies in the EMS. These were in part direct purchases of foreign currency by the Bundesbank; but marks were also paid into the EMCF for use in the intramarginal interventions.

Institutional arrangements, however, limited EMCF operations. No short-term loans of intervention currency were available from the European Fund, so for the most part the necessary mark funds had to be found through reduction of the Deutschmark reserves held by the central bank of the weak currency. These reserves were largely held on the market with prior approval by the Bundesbank. From July to the end of December 1986, intramarginal interventions of this kind had amounted to 16 billion marks, plus a further billion in mark reserves held by the Bundesbank.

Those interventions were 'fully effective' on German liquidity and reduced the holdings of foreign banks at the Bundesbank, although these were replenished as the effects of the sales on the price of marks came through.[14] These operations, however, underscored dissatisfaction with the financing of intramarginal interventions.

Reform: past, present and future

Debate on financing mechanisms for the EMS carried over into other areas. The agreement made by finance ministers in September 1987 at Nyborg grew out of dissatisfaction with the cost of interventions. The following year heads of government agreed to establish a Franco-German Economic Council, intended to increase coordination of monetary policy between the two countries. The most far-reaching development was the beginning of a plan to replace the EMS with a European Monetary Union. This was contained in the *Report on Economic and Monetary Union in the European Community* (the Delors Committee Report, described in greater detail below), which was delivered to the European heads of government at Madrid in June 1989. Each of these cases challenged the norms of the Bundesbank's policy and its position in the federal German system. The Bank proved to be a remarkably resilient political actor on the European scene, however, able to balance domestic obligations against the tensions of increasing international power.

Nyborg

At their meeting in Nyborg on 11–13 September 1987, European Finance Ministers announced a plan for EMS interventions to accommodate the position of weaker-currency countries. The Nyborg agreement allowed central banks whose currency came under pressure to borrow a strong currency from another central bank (in practice this meant borrowing marks from the Bundesbank). Moreover, short-term loans of this kind could be repaid in ecus – relieving the borrower of straight hard-currency debts once the operation was over. Disputes such as those accompanying the January 1987 realignment might have been avoided by this means, and proponents of the new scheme also saw it as representing a step towards increased international cooperation in decision-making.

Governments and central banks discussed the Nyborg agreement throughout the summer preceding its announcement. It was initially supported, according to Bonn sources, by Bundesbank President Pöhl; but when Hans Tietmeyer, then State Secretary in the Finance Ministry, went to Frankfurt for the CBC meeting on 27 August 1987 the Central Bank Council was sceptical. It refused to approve any kind of 'automatic' financing mechanism.[15] While other Europeans, notably the French, favoured the Nyborg plan, Bundesbank officials regarded the new financing proposals as an attempt to shake the foundations of German monetary policy.[16] Having overshot its corridor for 1985–6, the Bundesbank was still preoccupied by developments in the money supply in summer 1987. During this period of negotiations leading up to Nyborg the CBC saw the issue of financing exchange-rate intervention in the context of the domestic German money supply.

The Bundesbank's first criterion in reviewing its 1986–7 EMS operations was their effect on bank liquidity in the Federal Republic. Interventions could be 'advantageously' financed, as during the 1986–7 operations, as long as they did not carry lasting negative implications for domestic liquidity.[17] These advantages would be lost, the Bundesbank argued, should French demands for a 'very short-term financing arrangement to cover intramarginal interventions' be instituted. The Bank repeated its argument that it was seldom helpful to shore up a currency under severe market pressure. Such interventions would be more likely to increase EMS turbulence than calm it: market reaction to central bank intervention would encourage a weakening trend, raising the final costs of preserving EMS bands.[18] From the Bank's perspective, increasing convergence towards the Bundesbank standard and the model of the German economy was the only real solution.

Bundesbank officials were ultimately concerned to protect the Bank's position as defender of the currency in the face of a perceived international challenge. Any kind of 'automatic' financing plan would transfer monetary sovereignty to a supranational organization, and would mean in effect renunciation of the sort of autonomous policy-making position to which the Germans' economic position in Europe accustomed them. It abdicated, too, the Bundesbank's responsibilities in German public law.

The French, chafing at the effect that German stability norms had had on their economy in 1986, rejected the standard Bundesbank remedy of convergence towards such a norm. They wanted an automatic financing scheme for intramarginal interventions, and progress towards greater symmetry in the system. They also looked beyond the burden-sharing of intramarginal interventions towards reducing German trade surpluses.

This political constellation led to a coalition of France, Belgium and Italy (the weak-currency countries) on one side, opposed by strong-currency countries linked to the mark (Germany, the Netherlands and Denmark). The outcome at Nyborg was a 'gentlemen's agreement'. There would be strong-currency contributions to the European Monetary Cooperation Fund to finance intramarginal interventions, saving the reserves of the weak-currency countries. The repayment period was increased from two and a half to three months, with repayment in ecus permitted. It was also agreed that economic convergence should be more closely supervised in future.

Although Nyborg appeared to distribute EMS costs more equitably, different interpretations immediately appeared. Jacques de Larosier, head of the Banque de France, spoke of the Nyborg agreement as being 'presumably automatic'. Mark Eyskens, Belgian Finance Minister, said creditor central banks would bear the 'burden of proof' should they refuse the necessary credits at any time. French Finance Minister Edouard Balladur regarded Nyborg as realizing French proposals of the preceding February and 'a decisive step towards enhancing the EMS'. Bundesbank President Pöhl, expressing the CBC's view, asserted the creditor central bank's right to assess the monetary situation, including domestic factors, before committing any funds for intervention. Nyborg's main purpose, Pöhl said, was to reduce the cost of preserving established bands in the EMS. Denmark's central bank President Erik Hoffmeyer spoke of his hope that the total volume of intervention financing could be reduced 'through mutual agreement'.

In the three years since Nyborg, no financing requests for intramarginal interventions have been refused by the Bundesbank, yet its political position in the EMS remains remarkably untouched. Contrary to fears that Nyborg would undermine the Bank's autonomy, it now seems a successful example of a typical Bundesbank compromise in the European situation: having made a gesture towards international cooperation, the Bundesbank was able to protect its own position too.

The Franco-German Economic Council

Similarly, a mix of national interests and European ideals characterized the 1987 proposal for a Franco-German Economic Council. While monetary policy in both countries converged substantially, economic imbalances remained. Interest rates throughout the 1980s were significantly higher in France.[19] During 1986–7 Germany's trade surplus with France increased from 15.1 to 16.3 billion marks, with a similar rise in the German surplus in services (from 12.9 to 14.2 billion marks). Despite that imbalance, however, both countries achieved a remarkable degree of uniformity in growth and inflation rates. During 1987 their inflation differential fell from 3.8% to 1.7% and both economies grew by 2% over the year.[20]

Whereas Bundesbank analyses attribute this performance to disciplined monetary policy producing a tight parallel between interest rates in the core of low inflation countries, French commentators called the results of that system 'a German diktat'.[21] Policymakers there, chafing at limitations imposed by the Bundesbank standard on their national economic policy, hoped to achieve through inter-European cooperation what they had not secured alone or in bilateral negotiations: access to policy-making in the Bundesbank itself.

The Franco-German Council began as a political gesture by Helmut Kohl's CDU-FDP government to commemorate the 25th anniversary of the 1963 Franco-German Treaty on cooperation. A draft treaty negotiated during November 1987 committed both governments to create a new policy-coordination mechanism.[22]

'Economic coordination' and 'harmonization' of Franco-German economic policy were vague notions that French politicians were anxious to see made concrete through an institutional forum. The 1987 Treaty appeared a perfect instrument to pry loose the Bundesbank standard. The Council was expected to meet four times each year, alternately in France and Germany, to discuss economic policy.[23] Members would include the French and German Finance and Economics Ministers and the Presidents of both central banks. Although the Banque de France is legally subordinate to the French government, the Treaty placed both central banks on an equal footing and bound each to economic coordination objectives determined by the new Council. It ignored other important provisions of the Bundesbank Law, such as the policy authority of the CBC. Most importantly, from the Bundesbank's point of view, the Franco-German Treaty said nothing about a stability norm. Economic policy was to be coordinated, but around which monetary factor? German negotiators appeared content to leave such issues to the politics of the Council.[24]

The Bundesbank was excluded from the negotiations leading up

95

to the Treaty. Although informed of its original contents, the Bank was not consulted when at French insistence a document initially intended to be ceremonial suddenly became a binding treaty in international law. The CBC did not receive a copy of the document until the day before its scheduled signature in Paris (22 January 1988). Kohl's gesture of Franco-German friendship now took on a decidedly sour cast: the Bundesbank reacted with immediate suspicion, provoking an instant French response.

Sensing that the Franco-German Council would be a 'Trojan horse', the Bundesbank moved onto the offensive as soon as details of the new Treaty were made public. Three days after its publication in the federal government's official digest, a legal opinion on its provisions prepared by the Bundesbank's staff was leaked to the German press. The lawyers warned that the Treaty would break the 1957 Bundesbank Law and offered legal grounds for the Bank's fear that Franco-German economic coordination through the Council would seriously limit its autonomy.[25] 'Harmonization' offered a blatant lever on Bundesbank policy.

Discussion at the next CBC meeting (on 4 February) focused on the Bundesbank's legal position should the Treaty be ratified in its original form. After an exceptionally long session of five hours, President Pöhl rejected French complaints that the Bundesbank gave too little support to the franc on the exchange markets. To reaffirm the Bank's primary responsibility for monetary stability, Pöhl announced there would be no increase in money supply, which would be kept to its 3–6% corridor.

As the German Central Bank Council was meeting, Chancellor Kohl spoke to the Bundestag, effectively conceding the case against the Treaty. It was obvious to the government, he asserted, that neither the Bundesbank's autonomy nor its goal of defending the currency should be affected by the Franco-German Council.[26]

The next day, Bundesbank officials wrote to the Finance Ministry, laying out the Bank's concerns about the effect of the new Treaty on the Bank's legal position and demanding a binding assurance that the Treaty would not impinge on its autonomy. A spate of reports on the new Treaty appeared in the German press, generating publicity that ultimately strengthened the Bank's hand against the federal government. German observers agreed that the Treaty threatened the Bank's legal status, but there were divergent views on what should be done. New legislation to protect the Bundesbank's status in public law and appending a preamble affirming the Bank's independence to the Treaty draft were both discussed. The government finally chose to amend the Treaty.

In the struggle over the Franco-German Economic Council the Bundesbank used interest-group pressure and the persuasion of politicians sympathetic to its view to achieve its goal. Official statements on related issues, such as European monetary integration, reiterated the necessity of stable monetary policy for the domestic value of the mark and implied successfully that only the Bundesbank could be trusted with Germany's monetary policy.[27]

Although the Treaty changes demanded by the Bank were not formally completed until November 1988, its victory over the Kohl government was sealed in mid-June when the Chancellor attended a meeting of the Bundesbank CBC.[28] At the Franco-German Council's second meeting – this time in the Bundesbank headquarters at Frankfurt – the Bank was so confident of its position vis-à-vis the government in Bonn that it used the occasion to demonstrate its autonomy to the French.[29]

When legislation ratifying the Treaty on a Franco-German Economic Council finally reached the Bundestag in November, it explicitly declared that the Treaty did not limit the autonomy of the Bundesbank in any way. The Bundesbank could review its politics on the whole issue with satisfaction. Its suspicions of the 'Trojan horse' had, for a while at least, been set aside.

A European Central Bank

The future of monetary union in Europe dominated Community politics in 1988–9. The main impetus for a commission to study the steps towards a common currency and European Central Bank came from France, but, as in the case of negotiations over a Franco-German Economic Council, they found an ally in the German Foreign Minister.[30]

Hans-Dietrich Genscher went to the Hanover summit in 1988 already committed to the French proposal for a commission to study the practicality of monetary union. Chancellor Kohl accepted its symbolic importance, and saw the domestic utility of a European gesture in this area, hoping to repeat the success of Germany's EC presidency. Although tax harmonization had foundered, under German stewardship progress had been made in 1988 on the 1992 dossier. Foreign observers and even Kohl's usual critics counted his tenure as a success. Other regulatory changes moved towards common road-haulage policies (a risky change in domestic German politics), uniform construction standards, pharmaceutical and health standards, and 'educational diplomas' which would make professional qualifications freely transferable. 'Mr Kohl can hand over the chair to Greece next month', Commission President Jacques Delors remarked, 'with the knowledge that the single market has come almost to the point of no return.'[31]

Kohl gave himself high marks too. After the German presidency the Community was 'prepared for the future with a clear and rational structure', he asserted. Trying to balance European pressure for a big step towards European unification against powerful domestic considerations, Kohl cautioned that monetary union could come only at the end of a long road ahead. Genscher was less restrained. 'There is no getting around the creation of a central European bank', he told listeners of Hessische Rundfunk on the eve of the Hanover summit.[32]

Genscher and the French carried the day, and European heads of government agreed at Hanover on the appointment of a committee, chaired by Jacques Delors, to study monetary integration.[33] Its report to the Madrid summit of European heads of government a year later addressed four central questions: (1) Is a single European currency feasible? (2) Could the ecu serve that function? (3) What if a European central bank were to replace the national central banks, with responsibility for a single European currency? (4) If such steps were agreed, how might the transition be organized?

The *Report on Economic and Monetary Union in the European Community*[34] followed an agenda set by those questions and proposed that monetary union could be reached over three stages of development. The first, ending exchange controls and removing obstacles to European-wide banking, securities and insurance services, was already agreed for 1 July 1990. Over the next two stages a common currency and a regional central bank might be introduced, but the Report suggested no timetable for these. Beyond the first phase starting in 1990, European heads of government agreed only to set up another consultative body to prepare an intergovernmental conference on the subject sometime after 1990. The Committee added a statement of principle which Bundesbank President Pöhl called 'the most beautiful sentence in the document': a future European central bank must be independent both of national governments and the European Commission, and it must be bound to the norm of monetary stability.

In reaction the British Prime Minister, Margaret Thatcher, warned that, should the report be implemented, it would amount to 'the biggest transfer of national sovereignty we've ever had, and I don't think it will be at all acceptable to the British parliament'. President Mitterrand and Chancellor Kohl were as enthusiastic as the British were sceptical, with Jacques Delors remarking on British worries about national sovereignty that 'for the first time the right in the Community is more ideological than the left'.

While the Bundesbank was less outspoken on the impracticalities of monetary union than Mrs Thatcher, the Committee's report did not entirely still the fears of Germany's central bankers. Apart from welcoming the report's declaration of principle on independence and monetary stability, Bundesbank officials warned it would take many years before material convergence of the European economies could make monetary union practical.

Conclusion

In a single decade the EMS fulfilled its purpose of creating 'a zone of monetary stability in Europe'. But in other respects – equitable distribution of financial burdens and substantial convergence of the European economies – the system fell short of expectations. With the new impetus given monetary and economic union by the Delors Report, those aspects of the EMS remain volatile political issues.

An asymmetrical system?

EMS membership ties Germany's partners to the mark – and thus to the Bundesbank's monetary course. Dependence on the German currency has produced unwanted political effects for some EMS members, particularly France, and there have been recurrent demands that European 'asymmetry' be reduced.

The disagreement turns on German power in the EMS. At one level debate focuses on how a common goal, economic convergence, should be measured and attained. Complaints about present 'asymmetry' refer to national differentials of size, efficiency and productivity as well as differences in their balance-of-payments position. Demands for increased symmetry most often come from representatives of the weaker economies in the EMS, and the most important conflict stems from Franco-German imbalances.[35] France's persistently negative trade relationship with Germany spills over into the EMS by generating exchange-rate pressures which must be stabilized through market interventions and domestic deflation.

At another level the asymmetry issue is one of fairness. Full economic integration assumes that greater convergence can be achieved between countries with strong currencies and those whose currencies are weak. The question is whether interest and exchange rates should reflect divergent price and cost differentials or be used to further domestic fiscal and economic policy and the long-range goal of European integration.[36] Majority opinion in the Bundesbank, assuming that exchange rates must represent a country's underlying economic position, has argued against efforts to use monetary policy to further Europe's political goals.

The issue of asymmetry is not likely to go away despite the narrowing of intra-European differentials on such important economic indicators as inflation and interest rates. But political changes outside the European Community since the 'German autumn' of 1989 will make it harder for the Bundesbank to pursue its political line in future.

The burdens of intervention

Intramarginal transactions are now the Bundesbank's main concern. In the 1986–7 realignments, they had a greater impact on German liquidity than obligatory interventions in the EMS (see Table 5). There was a significant contractionary effect in 1986, as marks were purchased, and in 1987 sales of the German currency produced an increase of 18.1 billion marks. In both years targets for growth in the central bank money stock were overshot.

Do EMS transactions endanger the Bundesbank's control of the money supply? Theoretically, yes; in practice, no.[37] The EMS has made relatively little impact on the German money supply over the past ten years.[38] Nevertheless, severe short-term fluctuations in bank liquidity and money supply aggregates are caused by EMS interventions. Particularly in realignment periods, marginal and intramarginal interventions have caused marked changes in the Bundesbank's net external position.[39]

How, then, has its EMS role affected Bundesbank policy? While not seriously endangering control of the money supply in Germany,

Table 5 DM interventions in the EMS[1] (DM billion)

Calendar year	Mandatory	Intramarginal	Total	Effect on German liquidity
1979[2]				
Purchases	—	−2.7	−2.7	−2.4
Sales	+3.6	+8.1	+11.7	+11.7
Balance	+3.6	+5.4	+9.0	+9.2
1980				
Purchases	−5.9	−5.9	−11.8	−11.1
Sales	—	+1.0	+1.0	+0.6
Balance	−5.9	−4.9	−10.8	−10.5
1981				
Purchases	−2.3	−8.1	−10.4	−10.3
Sales	+17.3	+12.8	+30.1	+25.3
Balance	+15.0	+4.7	+19.7	+15.0
1982				
Purchases	—	−9.4	−9.4	−2.5
Sales	+3.0	+12.8	+15.8	+6.1
Balance	+3.0	+3.4	+6.4	+3.7
1983				
Purchases	−16.7	−19.1	−35.8	−20.4
Sales	+8.3	+12.9	+21.2	+12.6
Balance	−8.4	−6.2	−14.5	−7.8
1984				
Purchases	—	−30.2	−30.2	−0.8
Sales	+4.7	+7.6	+12.3	+4.4
Balance	+4.7	−22.7	−17.9	+3.6
1985				
Purchases	—	−29.6	−29.6	−0.2
Sales	+0.4	+30.8	+31.1	—
Balance	+0.4	+1.2	+1.5	−0.2
1986				
Purchases	−19.0	−33.6	−52.6	−12.1
Sales	+4.1	+76.0	+80.1	+3.8
Balance	−14.8	+42.4	+27.6	−8.4
1987				
Purchases	—	−48.1	−48.1	−7.3
Sales	+15.0	+62.7	+77.7	+25.4
Balance	+15.0	+14.6	+29.7	+18.1
1988				
Purchases	—	−28.2	−28.2	−6.1
Sales	—	+16.8	+16.8	—
Balance	—	−11.4	−11.4	−6.1

Notes: [1] DM interventions of other central banks participating in the EMS, and EMS interventions of the Bundesbank.
　　　[2] From the start of the EMS on 13 March 1979.
　　　+ = DM sales (expansionary effect on German liquidity).
　　　− = DM purchases (contractionary effect on German liquidity).
Sources: Deutsche Bundesbank, *Annual Report 1986, 1988*; H. Sherman, *Tokyo Club Papers*, no. 3, 1990.

EMS concerns do appear to affect interest-rate policy.[40] Just as interest rates in other EMS countries are influenced by their exchange-rate position (and thus Bundesbank policy), the mark's EMS role constrains German interest-rate movements.

Who pays?

Distributing the costs of monetary stability in Europe proved the most intractable EMS issue. Decreased fiscal and budgetary divergences contribute to monetary stability, but European governments and central banks still disagree on the next steps in the unification process. The 'economist' position taken by the Bundesbank and British government and the opposing 'monetarist' view of European economic integration advanced by France and the Latin countries reflect their different approaches and interests.[41] The cases of Nyborg and the Franco-German Economic Council are paradigm examples of how the Bundesbank used its power in the past to accommodate political pressures without relinquishing monetary hegemony in the EMS.

Who governs?

A Central Bank Council consensus exists on a model for the European central bank resembling their own institution, but there is less agreement on the question of market-led versus state-led economic integration.[42]

A CBC majority believes that a European central bank can come into existence only after substantial European financial and economic integration. The position of this majority conforms to established Bundesbank theory: real factors and forces drive the economy, and these are beyond the reach of monetary policy. Money and money supply *represent* a reality; they affect production and the real economy, but cannot substitute for other factors. Bundesbank practice treats price increases differentially within the stability paradigm. A smaller group, including Hamburg LCB President Wilhelm Nölling, accepts a version of the 'pacemaker' argument, viewing monetary union as a means to political unification.[43]

When Claus Köhler, speaking in Paris during October 1988, characterized the two approaches to monetary union as the 'leap in the dark' and the 'crowning theory', identifying successful EMS development as a product of 'leap in the dark' thinking, he sent a signal back to the Bundesbank's Central Council. Köhler's argument reminded his fellow central bankers of the Bundesbank's historically specific position. Should a European central bank be established, it will support political developments very different from the course of German history after 1945. Although his emphasis differs from Köhler's, Norbert Kloten has also suggested that the 'stability anchor' of the mark and the Bundesbank standard will give way to other powers and norms able 'to realize the forms of a democratic will in Europe'.[44]

The *Report on Economic and Monetary Union* did not end debate on Europe's monetary future: it marked out the terrain of the political struggle now just beginning. Barring an unlikely change in its statute, the German Bundesbank will continue to judge every plan for European monetary integration against its stability standard and take much the same approach as in the Nyborg case, in which it interpreted the ambiguities of the text to secure its own position. Defending domestic price stabilty will continue to be its first concern. That fact, combined with Germany's size, wealth and the asymmetric results of monetary *Realpolitik* (with appreciators having the power in this system), seem to secure the Bundesbank's present position as monetary hegemon of the European Community for the foreseeable future.

6

THE BUNDESBANK IN
A CHANGING WORLD

As the Bundesbank enters the 1990s it faces the familiar dilemma of maintaining its domestic priorities under increasing international pressures. The unification process itself is making the pursuit of domestic anti-inflation objectives more difficult. As the Bank strives to reconcile these conflicting domestic and international policies, what does its past lead us to expect of its future?

'Protecting the currency': an institutional identity
The cases of Bundesbank–government conflict analysed in previous chapters reveal three important dimensions of monetary policy in the Federal Republic: deeply-ingrained fear of inflation on the part of the German public; independent monetary authority backed by the normative power of law in domestic politics; and a constitutional decision in favour of federalism and a political decision in favour of the social market economy. How secure are these dimensions?

(i) Monetary stability
For more than three decades, the institutional character of Germany's central bank has been defined by its legal norm: 'protecting the currency' has meant preventing inflation. That criterion of monetary policy was assured by the lessons the West German public drew from their history in this century. For a democratic electorate that remembered catastrophic inflations in the Weimar Republic and after the Second World War, the Deutschmark's success after

1948 added legitimacy to the central bank's policy claims. Those experiences translated into an exceptional public sensibility to price inflation. Although there are some indications of change in their 'inflation psychology', West German workers still seem more willing than their European neighbours to limit wage demands when price increases are controlled. As monetary and economic union between the two Germanies takes effect, there are signs that workers in the eastern Länder are not so disciplined and that, for them, wage demands may come before monetary stability.[1] In addition to the potential discrepancy between East and West German 'stability consciousness', financing the economic restructuring in the east will certainly strain German monetary management.[2] That could produce a conflict between government and the central bank which would overshadow all the cases discussed above.

(*ii*) *Independence*
The Bundesbank Act of 1957 defined the Bank's independent status and anti-inflationary policy standard as a fundamental norm, and West German political culture accepted and understood the need for its relatively autonomous monetary authority. Between 1949 and 1989 a succession of Chancellors in the Federal Republic discovered that an independent central bank could significantly constrain their domestic policy and the pursuit of international economic objectives. Whatever the economic consequences for West Germans, none of the cases discussed above damaged the Bundesbank's prestige or affected substantially its position in German public opinion.[3] However, the move towards a European central bank with the Bundesbank as only one – albeit potentially the most powerful – of its regional arms would reduce the Bank's independence more than any previous moves towards monetary integration in Europe.

(*iii*) *Federalism and the social market economy*
Determined reformers made these two principles the basis of a new constitutional order in West Germany after 1945. The Basic Law, an arrangement intended to be provisional when it was promulgated in 1949, established what proved to be the most durable democracy in the country's history. The federal redistribution of costs and incomes gave its profitable economy a system of social justice without stifling productivity or capital opportunity. Part of the story of the Bundesbank's security at home and monetary success has

105

been its ability to persuade Germans that domestic growth cannot be pursued at the expense of stable money.

For a non-elected governmental body charged with highly political responsibilities, the Bundesbank's conformity to the general pattern of federal structures in West Germany added a necessary element of representativeness to its policy-making. While concentrating decision-making in the Central Council, the framers of the Bundesbank Act nevertheless distributed CBC membership among the Länder and gave final power over its appointments to elected officials throughout Germany. Without those aspects of political representation, it is unlikely that such as essentially elitist institution could have attained its present position in German politics. Domestic pressures for an expansionary monetary policy to ease the pain of economic restructuring in a unified Germany, or the establishment of a 'Eurofed' less sensitive to German concerns, could begin to undermine traditional support for the stability norm.

Policy parameters: what does inflation mean?

The rhetoric of Bundesbank policy has until now presented a simplified view of inflation to the public imagination. Anti-inflationary policy can thus appear as a relatively uncomplicated refusal to compromise, despite the complex relationship between the monetary and real economies. The Bank's public message, often reiterated, claims that 'there is no such thing as a little bit of inflation' and that even single-digit inflation destroys a currency's value over the medium term and gradually destroys the economy as a whole. In the words of Bundesbank Vice-President Helmut Schlesinger, stable currency is 'the precondition of a functioning market economy and economic growth'.

The Bundesbank's working definition of inflation, as we have seen, is rather different. It determines an 'unavoidable' rate of inflation by reference to underlying trends. When German monetary policy is being made, the question of inflationary pressures is open to interpretation. The German pursuit of stability does not depend on a simply conceived monetary variable, but on an economically complex measure for changes in the money supply based on expected growth in nominal national income and velocity of circulation. 'Sound money' therefore is the expression of a *normative* criterion for the development of Germany's domestic economy, and 'inflation' is seen as deviation from that norm, which remains constant.

The Bundesbank's institutional character, then, and its policy approach, reflect the realities of the German economy. It always remains focused on these two factors, without which neither the Bank's ethos nor its monetary standard would be meaningful. That more normative approach may be easier to manage in a 'Eurofed' than a simple reference to Bundesbank rhetoric suggests.

The processes of integration

While the Bundesbank retains its domestic focus, the Federal Republic of Germany has become a regional and global power. The foremost economic nation in Europe, Germany successfully allies its foreign policy interests in the European Community to those of its main trading partners. This has meant a close relationship with the French from the beginning, and between them, France and Germany hold the keys to economic and political integration in Europe. Though a vital strategic territory after 1945, the Federal Republic took a back seat to the 'special relationship' between America and Britain for most of the postwar period. Under the presidency of George Bush, however, Germany appears to be displacing Britain as the main Western partner of the United States, although its inability to send troops to the Persian Gulf in 1990 after the Iraqi invasion of Kuwait has meant a more strained relationship with this new partner than the United States enjoyed with Britain. Nevertheless, without American approval the momentum for German unification after November 1989 might well have been slowed by European doubts.

Those processes of international change now ensnare the Bundesbank, and carry profound implications for its position in a new Germany and a new Europe. Some of these processes have been explored above: the liberalization of capital markets and volatile exchange-rate structures which forge sometimes unwanted linkages between the Bank's domestic monetary factors and the economies of other nations. Two hold the possibility of revolutionary changes in store: the prospect of European Monetary Union, and the reality of German Economic, Social and Monetary Union (GEMU).

(i) European Monetary Union

As discussed in Chapter 5, the Bundesbank won on many of the issues facing the Delors Commission in 1988–9. A future central bank for a common European currency will look much like the Bundesbank, following its model of independence from government and dedication to monetary policy. If present trends continue, Europe's central bank will also be federal, distributing its policy-making powers throughout the Community, with representatives from all its members on the central council. The conceptual path towards monetary union in Europe already bears clear signs of Bundesbank influence. That and the Bundesbank's power in Europe increase the prospects that, however phase three of the Delors Committee's recommendation is implemented, it will succeed only if it meets the Bundesbank's demands for a 'Eurofed' much like itself.

In the present phase of monetary integration, the Bundesbank won an important point in having Karl Otto Pöhl appointed to chair the committee considering what to do next. This part of the Delors Committee's remit is so vaguely drawn and offers so many possible interpretations that the German central bank will be able to find sufficient grounds to keep the matter under discussion for a very long time. Given its skill in reading European doctrine – especially when it comes to the fine points of monetary integration – the Bundesbank is poised to interpret (and reinterpret) the final Eurofed document until the contents suit its own norm of monetary stability. President Pöhl recently chose a highly visible forum to express Bundesbank misgivings about the speed of monetary union in Europe, declaring that he still had 'serious doubts that European governments, not just the British government, are really prepared to accept the consequences of a transfer of far-reaching powers over monetary policy to a supranational institution'. Nothing would be quite as sound or secure as the Deutschmark had been, Pöhl implied: 'There's enormous suspicion here . . . that any other system would be weaker than the system we now have.' When ministers met in December 1990 to discuss phase two of monetary integration in Europe, Pöhl indicated, they would have only two choices – a real central bank (a Eurofed that acts like the Bundesbank) or a compromise that would negate everything the Germans stood for in monetary policy.[4]

Formal guarantees of stability only approximate the Bundesbank's practice, however, the success of which depends on a domestic political culture specific to the Federal Republic of Germany and unlikely to be replicated elsewhere. Should Eurofed become a reality, what means would the Germans have available to pursue their style of monetary management within such a body? Basically two: the power of the Germany economy in an integrated European context, and the educative influence of an independent central bank on the politics of other European countries.

In the politics of committee work leading up to such a drastic change in Europe, the cases of Nyborg and the Franco-German Economic Council, examined in Chapter 5, offer evidence of how firmly the Bundesbank has held onto its domestic orientation, judging every plan for integration (whether consultation, cooperation or coordination) by its own standard. Its policies remain firmly rooted in a domestic frame of reference. Until there is a European central bank, international processes will continue to provoke a search for flexible institutional responses which preserve the maximum feasible degree of Bundesbank autonomy.

(ii) German Economic, Social and Monetary Union
The Treaty between the Federal Republic and the German Democratic Republic that came into effect on 1 July 1990 and marked the beginning of German unification has already enhanced the Bundesbank's domestic perspective. Though anxious not to suggest an obvious conflict between the goals of European integration and German unification, the Bundesbank, like all institutions of German government, faces a difficult task of setting national priorities and balancing those against European and international commitments.[5] German monetary and economic union is different from European integration in one important respect: the eastern Länder have now been absorbed legally by the Federal Republic and, unlike Europe's nation-states, the sovereignty of the German Democratic Republic was already partly extinguished when the GEMU came into effect. But the political and financial demands German unification will make on Germany's wealth and political culture are far greater than those it has yet faced from the pressures of European unity. How will the Bundesbank fare in these new circumstances?

Despite its apparent loss to the federal government in February 1990 over a monetary union which Bundesbank President Pöhl called 'fantastic' only days before it was announced in Bonn, the Bundesbank won on a major aspect of the plan. Its opposition to the 1:1 exchange of East German marks for the Deutschmark hinted at by Helmut Kohl during the East German elections of March 1990 led to the acceptance of the Bundesbank's recommendation for an exchange rate of 2:1 for holdings above 4,000 Ostmarks. The Bank lost on the issue of a currency union between two very different economies, being forced to bow in the domestic political debate to the realities of the unique national opportunity defined by the CDU-FDP government. At least in this case, one variant of the 'leap in the dark theory' replaced the 'crowning theory'. When the Bundesbank was put in charge of monetary policy for the whole of the east, it stressed its standard of 'sound money' in the weeks preceding the introduction of the Deutschmark in the GDR. Now that monetary union is complete, it has reverted to a modified version of the 'crowning theory', stressing the need to keep wages in line with productivity in East German enterprises, but accepting that only a radical break with the socialist economic system could liberate the forces of capital creation and productivity on which a rebuilt social system in the eastern Länder depends.[6]

Now that Germany is reunited, there are no signs of significant change in the Bundesbank paradigm for monetary management. On the contrary: reviewing its work in 1989 and looking forward to the demands of unification, the Bundesbank offered a familiar analysis of the situation Germany would soon face: an 'exposed flank' (inflationary pressures from outside) and domestic demand that exceeded capacity (inflationary pressures from within). In order to manage those demands within the Bundesbank paradigm, interest rates and the external value of the mark would have to stay high. Wages and prices in the east had to be 'realistic' (in line with economic fundamentals) and – most importantly from the Bank's perspective – restructuring should not be financed through new credit. German unity, so the Bundesbank's prescription reads, cannot be borrowed against future productivity, but must be paid for now through savings and taxes.[7]

Chancellor Helmut Kohl's promise of 'no new taxes' is unlikely to be kept in the face of such clear warnings from the German central bank. In any further case of Bundesbank–government conflict such as those discussed above, the Bank can be confident of its position. Fiscal policies to finance new investment or increases in social payments which it considers risky would be likely to be frustrated by the Bundesbank's monetary instruments, much as were Helmut Schmidt's efforts to stimulate the German economy in 1981. But the stakes were never as high as they have been over German unification. In midsummer 1990, Karl Otto Pöhl reminded Germans (and particularly critics in the SPD) that unity was a categorically different question from other policy issues, one that could not be mastered if the focus remained on the question: 'how much will it cost me?'

But the question of cost is already on the Bundesbank's agenda. In the struggle with the German government now shaping up over the answer and the money to pay the bill, the final say belongs to the Deutsche Bundesbank.

NOTES

Chapter 1

1 Guy Kirsch, 'Politische Grenzen der Geldpolitik', in W. Ehrlicher and D.B. Simmert (eds.), *Geld- und Währungspolitik in der Bundesrepublik Deutschland* (Berlin: Duncker and Humblot, 1982).
2 It goes far beyond the scope of this study to consider in any depth the role of normative argument in politics, but see Friedrich V. Kratochwil, *Rules, Norms and Decisions: On the Conditions of Practical and Legal Reasoning in International and Domestic Affairs* (Cambridge: Cambridge University Press, 1989) on the resort to norms in order to adduce reasons for action.

Chapter 2

1 See *Deutsches Geld- und Bankwesen in Zahlen* (Frankfurt: Deutsche Bundesbank, 1976), p. 25; Werner Abelshauser, *Wirtschaftsgeschichte der Bundesrepublik Deutschland* (Frankfurt: Suhrkamp, 1983).
2 Gordon Craig, *Germany, 1866–1945* (Oxford: Clarendon Press, 1978), pp. 450–1. See also Gerald D. Feldman (ed.), *Die Deutsche Inflation: Eine Zwischenbilanz. Beiträge zu Inflation und Wiederaufbau in Europa, 1914–1924* (Berlin: de Gruyter, 1982).
3 Craig, *Germany*, p. 435.
4 Gerold Ambrosius, *Die Durchsetzung der sozialen Marktwirtschaft in Westdeutschland 1948–1954* (Stuttgart: Klett-Cotta, 1977).
5 Frank Vogel, *German Business after the Economic Miracle* (London: Macmillan, 1973) p. 5.
6 Helmut Schlesinger, 'Kontinuität in den Zielen, Wandel in den Methoden', in Wolfgang Filc, Lothar Hübl and Rüdiger Pohl (eds.),

Herausforderungen der Wirtschaftspolitik. Festschrift zum 60. Geburtstag von Claus Köhler (Berlin: Duncker and Humblot, 1988), p. 197.

7 K. O. Pöhl, 'Eine konsequente Stabilitätspolitik hat uns das Vertrauen des Auslands erhalten', Deutsche Bundesbank, *Auszüge aus Presseartikeln*, no. 45, 20 June 1988.

8 E. Noelle-Neumann, 'Geldwert und öffentliche Meinung. Anmerkungen zur "Psychologie der Inflation"', in C. A. Andreae, K. H. Hansmeyer and G. Scherhorn, *Geldtheorie und Geldpolitik. Gustav Schmölders zum 65. Geburtstag* (Berlin: Duncker and Humblot, 1968), p. 37.

9 J. Jeske, 'Stabilität – nur ein schönes Wort?', *Frankfurter Allgemeine Zeitung*, 16 November 1985.

10 Gordon Smith, *Democracy in Western Germany: Parties and Politics in the Federal Republic* (London: Heinemann, 1979), pp. 68–9.

11 British Military Government Ordinance No. 129.

12 Deutsche Bundesbank, *30 Jahre Deutsche Bundesbank. Die Entstehung des Bundesbankgesetzes vom 26. Juli 1957* (Frankfurt: Deutsche Bundesbank, 1988).

13 Bundesbank Law (*Bundesbankgesetz*, BBkG) paras. 12 and 3. See also the authoritative commentary by Joachim v. Spindler, Willy Becker and Ernest Starke, *Die Deutsche Bundesbank. Grundzüge des Notenbankwesens und Kommentar zum Gesetz über die Deutsche Bundesbank* (Stuttgart: Verlag W. Kohlhammer, 1973), pp. 256ff. (for para. 12) and pp. 192ff. (for para. 3).

14 In September 1985 finance ministers and central bank presidents from the G-5 nations (France, West Germany, Japan, the United Kingdom and the United States) met at the Plaza Hotel in New York and issued a call to the markets to bring the value of the US dollar into line with fundamentals affecting exchange rates. When the G-5 group met in Paris during February 1987, they followed the 'Plaza communiqué' of 1985 with a stronger declaration on exchange rates in February 1987, the 'Louvre Accord'. See Peter B. Kenen, *Managing Exchange Rates* (London: Routledge/RIIA, 1988), p. 3, and I.M. Destler and C. Randall Henning, *Dollar Politics: Exchange Rate Policymaking in the United States* (Washington, DC: Institute for International Economics, 1989).

15 Roland Sturm, 'The Role of the Bundesbank in German Politics', *West European Politics*, vol. 12, no. 2 (1989), p. 2.

16 B. Blohm, 'Und ewig lockt das Geld. Durch Pfundenwirtschaft verkommt das deutsche Zentralbankwesen', *Die Zeit*, No. 42, 9 October 1987.

17 'The political parties shall participate in the forming of the political will of the people.' Art. 21, Basic Law of the Federal Republic of Germany.

18 Rolf Caesar, *Der Handlungsspielraum der Notenbanken* (Baden-Baden: Nomos, 1981), p. 187.

19 Speech by Karl Otto Pöhl at the Central Bank of Lower Saxony in Hanover, 31 October 1988.

20 For the Bundesbank's assessment of the costs of German unity, see Hans Tietmeyer, 'The Economic Integration of Germany – Problems and Prospects', *Auszüge aus Presseartikeln*, no. 77, 2 October 1990.

21 Rolf Caesar, *Der Handlungsspielraum*, p. 170.

22 So-called after the 1944 conference held at Bretton Woods which set up a system (based on the dollar's convertibility to gold) that governed international exchange-rate policy until the early 1970s. See Benjamin J. Cohen, *Organizing the World's Money: The Political Economy of International Monetary Relations* (New York: Basic Books, 1977); John Williamson, *The Failure of World Monetary Reform, 1971–74* (New York: Council on Foreign Relations, 1977).

23 'Mid-February saw massive inflows of foreign exchange from EMS countries which led to an unwelcome increase in bank liquidity.' *Report of the Deutsche Bundesbank for the Year 1983*, p. 33.

24 For Pöhl's remarks, see 'Dollar Unity in Jeopardy', *Wall Street Journal*, 11 May 1989; and 'Massive Intervention Slows Dollar's Rise', *Wall Street Journal*, 19 May 1989. Representative of Leonard Gleske's position on managing exchange rates is his article, 'Monetary Policy: Priorities and Limitations', *International Monetary Cooperation: Essays in Honor of Henry C. Wallich* (Princeton, NJ: Dept. of Economics, Essays in International Finance No. 169, 1987).

25 Norbert Kloten, 'Die Steuerung des Geldmarktes als Reflex monetärer Konzeptionen', in Filc et al., *Herausforderungen*.

26 v. Spindler et al., *Die Deutsche Bundesbank*, p. 18.

27 Ibid, p. 19.

28 Claus Köhler, *Geldwirtschaft* (Berlin: Duncker and Humblot, several volumes, 1977–1983).

29 On the Keynesian foundations of the Stability and Growth Law, see Jeremiah M. Riemer, 'Alterations in the Design of Model Germany: Critical Innovations in the Policy Machinery for Economic Steering', in Andrei S. Markovits (ed.), *The Political Economy of West Germany* (New York: Praeger, 1982); and Christopher S. Allen, 'The Underdevelopment of Keynesianism in the Federal Republic of Germany', in Peter A. Hall (ed.), *The Political Power of Economic*

Ideas: Keynesianism across Nations (Princeton, NJ: Princeton
University Press, 1989).
30 Kloten, 'Steuerung des Geldmarktes', p. 186.
31 Gordon Smith, *Democracy in Western Germany*, p. 113.
32 Kloten, 'Steuerung des Geldmarktes', p. 185.
33 *The Deutsche Bundesbank: Its Monetary Policy Instruments and
Functions* (Frankfurt: Deutsche Bundesbank Special Series No. 7:
N.d.); Horst Seeck and Gernot Steffens, *Die Deutsche Bundesbank*
(Düsseldorf: Droste Verlag, 1979).
34 Christoph Buchheim, 'Die Bundesrepublik in der Weltwirtschaft', in
Wolfgang Benz (ed.), *Die Geschichte der Bundesrepublik Deutschland*,
vol. 2 (Frankfurt: Fischer, 1989), p. 198.
35 A question that may determine the success or failure of any future
Central European Bank, as the discussion in Chapter 5 indicates.

Chapter 3

1 See K. Stern's authoritative *Das Staatsrecht der Bundesrepublik
Deutschland*, vol. II, (Munich: C.H. Beck, 1980), especially
pp. 463–508; his argument summarizes this view. See also
C.-Th. Samm, *Die Stellung der Deutschen Bundesbank im
Verfassungsgefüge* (Berlin: Duncker and Humblot, 1967);
D. Uhlenbruck, *Die Verfassungsmässige Unabhängigkeit der
Deutschen Bundesbank und ihre Grenzen* (Munich: Beck, 1968).
A persuasive argument to the contrary is Reiner Schmidt, 'Die
Zentralbank im Verfassungsgefüge der Bundesrepublik
Deutschland', in Rolf Grawert (ed.), *Instrumente der sozialen
Sicherung und der Währungssicherung in der Bundesrepublik
Deutschland und in Italien* (Berlin: Duncker and Humblot, 1981)
p. 64. For a useful summary in English, see Carl-Ludwig
Holtfrerich, 'Relations between Monetary Authorities and
Governmental Institutions: the Case of Germany from the 19th
Century to the Present', in Gianni Toniolo (ed.), *Central Banks'
Independence in Historical Perspective* (Berlin and New York: de
Gruyter, 1988), pp. 105–59.
2 The processes of a 'social market economy' have not been without
political tension. See J. Donges, 'Industrial Politics in West
Germany's not so Market-oriented Economy', *World Politics*, no. 3
(1980); Kenneth Dyson, 'The Politics of Corporate Crisis in West
Germany', *West European Politics*, vol. 7 (1984). On the intellectual
origins of the social market economy, see Ludwig Erhard, *Deutsche
Wirtschaftspolitik: der Weg der sozialen Marktwirtschaft* (Düsseldorf:
Econ, 1962).

3 See Kenneth Dyson, 'Banks, State and Industry in West Germany', in A. Cox (ed.), *State, Banks and Industrial Finance* (Brighton: Wheatsheaf, 1985).

4 Para. 12, BBkG; v. Spindler, et al., *Die Deutsche Bundesbank*, p. 258. See also P. Stern-Münch and K.-H. Hansmeyer, *Das Gesetz zur Förderung der Stabilität und des Wachstums der Wirtschaft* (Stuttgart-Köln: Kohlhammer, 1971).

5 Interview with Dr Günter Schmölders, 'Rat der Wissenschaftler hat politische Beschlüsse nie ernsthaft beeinflußt', *Handelsblatt*, 8 July 1985. For an international comparison, see Henry C. Wallich, 'The American Council of Economic Advisors and the German *Sachverständigenrat*: a Study in the Politics of Economic Advice', *Economics* (August 1968), pp. 349–79.

6 For example, Dieter Kämpe, 'Überflüssiger Rat', *Der Spiegel*, 13 November 1988; 'Konjunktur-Experten: Magisches Karriere-Viereck', *Frankfurter Rundschau*, 18 November 1988.

7 The most recent example concerned sales of the Leopold tank to Saudi Arabia. After intense debate, the arms agreement had to be cancelled. Art. 24 (Basic Law) further complicates the issue; it enjoins the Federation to exercise its sovereignty to bring about 'a peaceful and lasting order in Europe and between the peoples of the world'. The provision has usually been interpreted as proscribing sales of arms to disturbed areas of the world.

8 Volker Berghahn, *Modern Germany. Society, Economy and Politics in the Twentieth Century* (Cambridge: Cambridge University Press, 1982), pp. 229–30.

9 'The German people ... have enacted, by virtue of their constituent power, this Basic Law for the Federal Republic of Germany. They have also acted on behalf of those Germans to whom participation was denied. The entire German people are called upon to achieve in free self-determination the unity and freedom of Germany.' *Basic Law*, Preamble. See also Rudolf Dolzer, 'Reunification and European Integration', manuscript delivered at the American Center for Contemporary German Studies, Johns Hopkins University, Washington, DC, 23 October 1989.

10 The classic discussion remains Gert von Eynern, *Die Unabhängigkeit der Notenbank* (Berlin: Colloquium Verlag, 1957). More recently: Hans-Joachim Arndt, 'Von der politischen zur plangebundenen Autonomie', in D. Duwendag (ed.), *Macht und Ohnmacht der Bundesbank* (Frankfurt: Athenäum Verlag, 1973); Rolf Caesar, 'Die Unabhängigkeit der Notenbank im demokratischen Staat. Argumente und Gegenargumente', *Zeitschrift für Politik*, vol. 25, (1978), pp. 347–69; Guy Kirsch, 'Politische Grenzen der Geldpolitik' (see above, Ch. 1, n. 1).

11 The exchange was reprinted in Deutsche Bundesbank, *W. Vocke zum 100. Geburtstag* (1986).

12 The government's veto power over Bundesbank policy is limited to suspending the Bank's decisions for a fortnight, so its effect is largely symbolic. The fact that this power has never been used of course intensifies a threat to use it, signalling such extreme disagreement with Bank policy that a government is prepared to violate a major political convention.

   A similar conflict between Bundesbank President Karl Klasen and Economics Minister Karl Schiller just before the 1972 general election had a different outcome. At the time the mark was under considerable external pressure in anticipation of its revaluation. Schiller wanted to stop the unwelcome inflow of foreign capital by increasing the value of the mark. Klasen wanted to apply the foreign capital through a tax on the purchase of German bonds and other securities. The cabinet voted to accept the Bundesbank's view over that of the Economics Minister – an unprecedented move in the history of the Federal Republic. Three days later, Schiller resigned. See Gerd Bucerius, 'Karl Klasen zum Achtzigsten. Der ehemalige Bundesbankpräsident war eine der wirtschaftspolitischen Leitfiguren der Nachkriegszeit', *Die Zeit*, 21 April 1989.

13 On the fall of the Schmidt government, see Arnuf Baring, *Machtwechsel* (Stuttgart: Deutsche Verlagsanstalt, 1982). A comparative analysis of economic policy in the SPD-FDP period is offered by Fritz W. Scharpf, *Sozialdemokratische Krisenpolitik in Europa*, (Frankfurt and New York: Campus Verlag, 1987).

14 The system broke down in stages. The United States ended dollar to gold conversion in August 1971 and in December of that year the mark was revalued in the Smithsonian Agreement. European currencies began to float against the dollar in March 1974. See Joanne Gowa, *Closing the Gold Window* (Ithaca, NY: Cornell University, 1983).

15 Robert D. Putnam and Nicholas Bayne, *Hanging Together. Cooperation and Conflict in the Seven-Power Summits* (London: Sage/RIIA, 1987), p. 92. This study provides a very clear summary of the events described below.

16 Quoted in ibid., p. 130.

17 Deutsche Bundesbank, *40 Jahre Deutsche Mark. Monetäre Statistiken 1948-1987* (Frankfurt: Deutsche Bundesbank, 1988), pp. 4–5, and 'Government Finance', in International Monetary Fund, *International Financial Statistics* (Washington: IMF, 1989), p. 156.

18 *Der Spiegel*, March 1981. For a brief overview of the political consequences of social changes in Germany during the 1980s see

Notes

Gerard Braunthal, 'Public Order and Civil Liberties', in Gordon Smith, William E. Patterson and Peter H. Merkl, *Developments in West German Politics* (London: Macmillan, 1989), pp. 308–22.

19 Stewart Fleming, 'Bundesbank likely to raise the Lombard rate', *The Financial Times*, 19 February 1981. The events of the next few weeks are well documented in the *Financial Times* and the *Frankfurter Allgemeine Zeitung*.

20 'Fest bleiben', *Frankfurter Allgemeine Zeitung*, 14 March 1981.

21 Erich Erlenbach, 'Die Tücken der "Abschnittsfinanzierung" werden offenbar. Wenn in einer Hochzinsphase Kredit benötigt wird. Das Zinsänderungsriziko', *Frankfurter Allgemeine Zeitung*, 3 April 1981.

22 'Bonner Investitionsanreize im Energiesektor. Erste Umrisse eines neuen Konjunktur- und Haushaltspaketes', *Neue Züricher Zeitung*, 5–6 April 1981. The Bundesbank considered Franco-German plans nothing less than an 'inflation alliance'. See the later report 'Inflations-allianz', *Frankfurter Allgemeine Zeitung*, 18 July 1981.

23 *Report of the Deutsche Bundesbank for the Year 1980*, pp. 1, 13, 26ff. The conflict between government and the Bundesbank remained a focus of political commentary in April and May 1981. See the long report in the *Frankfurter Allgemeine Zeitung*, 'Die Bundesrepublik hat aus der Substanz gelebt. Die Bundesbank berichtet über den Status der Auslandsvermögen und die Finanzierungsströme', 20 May 1981.

24 Reported in the *Frankfurter Allgemeine Zeitung*, 'Im Haushalt spiegelt sich alles wie in einem Brennglas. Was der Bundesbankpräsident den Politikern vorwirft', 3 June 1981.

25 John Tagliabue, 'Pöhl Critical of Bonn Policy', *International Herald Tribune*, 5 August 1981. The conflict over interest rates in 1981 produced lasting animosity between Helmut Schmidt and Karl Otto Pöhl, and Schmidt frequently blamed the fall of his government on the Bundesbank. In retrospect, Pöhl saw this incident as a particularly critical example of the 'tense relationship' between government and the Bundesbank that can arise over interpretation of general economic goals and monetary stability. The conclusion he draws today is hardly surprising in the context of the Bank's self-definition: 'The autonomy of the Bundesbank was preserved during this very difficult period of federal German history. It demonstrated that this autonomy need not conflict with fruitful cooperation with the federal government.' Pöhl, 'Widersprüche und Gemeinsamkeiten in der Politik der Bundesregierung und der Deutschen Bundesbank in der Zeit von 1978–1982', in Helmut Schmidt and Walter Hesselbach (eds.), *Kämpfer ohne Pathos. Festschrift für Hans Matthöfer zum 60. Geburtstag am 25. September 1985* (Bonn: Verlag Neue Gesellschaft, 1985), pp. 222–25.

Chapter 4

1 'Wall St. collapses as industrials plunge record 508.32 points', *Wall Street Journal*, 20 October 1987.

2 Baker's statement implied the Germans were undermining the Plaza agreement of the previous September. 'Die Deutschen sollen mitziehen', *Handelsblatt*, 8 January 1986.

3 Otmar Emminger, 'The D-Mark in the Conflict between Internal and External Equilibrium', *Essays in International Finance*, No. 122, (Princeton, NJ: Princeton University Department of Economics, International Finance Section, 1977), p. 1.

4 *40 Jahre Deutsche Mark*, p. 5 (see above, Ch. 3, n. 17).

5 Ibid, p. 10.

6 Emminger argued in retrospect that there had been relative calm for the mark because US prices and costs stayed steady during 1960–65 and the Americans' balance of payments improved as a result. Over this period, however, 'there was a steep rise in American capital exports which was not covered fully by the current-account surplus', resulting in exported inflation from America. Emminger, 'The D-Mark', p. 18.

7 Caesar, *Der Handlungsspielraum der Notenbanken*, p. 212.

8 Putnam and Bayne, *Hanging Together*, p. 29. Also Dieter Rebentisch, 'Gipfeldiplomatie und Weltökonomie: Weltwirtschaftliches Krisenmanagement während der Kanzlerschaft Helmut Schmidts 1974–1982', *Archiv für Sozialgeschichte*, vol. 28 (1988), pp. 307–32.

9 Putnam and Bayne, *Hanging Together*, p. 31. A particularly useful study of the relationship between economic policy and security from the German perspective is Helga Haftendorn, *Sicherheit und Stabilität: Außenbeziehungen der Bundesrepublik zwischen Ölkrise und Nato-Doppelbeschluß* (Munich: Beck, 1986).

10 'We have played our little part to keep the world economically together in a time when the larger economies, with wrong leadership from their respective governments, could quite easily have lapsed into the beggar-my-neighbour policies of the early 1930s ... There are still enormously strong tendencies for protectionism of all kinds... the so-called economic summit conferences helped to avoid that ... they did not bring about much, but what they avoided was of enormous importance.' Helmut Schmidt, *Weltwirtschaftsgipfel* (Bonn: Deutsche Gesellschaft für Auswärtige Politik, 1983), quoted in *The Economist*, 29 September 1979.

11 Putnam and Bayne, *Hanging Together*, p. 38. Also Helmut Schmidt, *Menschen und Mächte* (Berlin: Siedler Verlag, 1987), pp. 194–6.

12 Putnam and Bayne, *Hanging Together*, pp. 79–82.

13 Rebentisch, 'Gipfeldiplomatie und Weltökonomie', p. 320.

14 See Wolfgang Jäger and Werner Link, *Republik im Wandel: Die Ära Schmidt*, vol. 5 of *Geschichte der Bundesrepublik Deutschland* (Stuttgart: Deutsche Verlags Anstalt, 1987); and Putnam and Bayne, *Hanging Together*, p. 81, who describe the Bank's agreement as 'covering the Chancellor's right flank' and attribute the bankers' capitulation to international pressures.

15 Putnam and Bayne, *Hanging Together*, p. 198.

16 The uncertainty deliberately created by the G-5 ministers led to a fall of 12.5% in its value over the next half-year. See Yoichi Funabashi, *Managing the Dollar* (Washington, DC: Institute for International Economics, 1988); Putnam and Bayne, *Hanging Together*, p. 238.

17 They were as resistant to 'taking up the slack' for Treasury Secretary Baker as they had been to acting as 'locomotives' for Carter. Funabashi's description of Bundesbank policy after Plaza as 'refusing to be dictated to like the Bank of Japan' captures the Germans' sense of political independence from the Americans. Funabashi, *Managing the Dollar*, pp. 60–63.

18 *Welt am Sonntag*, 29 December 1985.

19 'Stabilität – nur ein schönes Wort?', *Frankfurter Allgemeine Zeitung*, 16 November 1985.

20 'Die Eins vor der Komma', *Bayernkurier*, 16 November 1985.

21 v. Spindler et al., *Die Deutsche Bundesbank*, p. 98. A useful cross-section of contemporary economic opinion on floating and the alternatives is offered by the extended series, 'Auf der Suche nach Alternativen zum Floating. Die internationale Währungsordnung im Umbruch', *Neue Züricher Zeitung*, 7–8 August to 16–17 October 1988.

22 Caesar, *Der Handlungsspielraum der Notenbanken*, p. 213.

23 *Report of the Deutsche Bundesbank for the Year 1986*, p. 32.

24 Ibid., p. 34.

25 Ibid., p. 17. The Bank's warnings on inflation at the time Germany reached 'deflationary' price levels are typical of its use of inflation rhetoric in the international sphere. See Helmut Schlesinger's comments at the end of July: 'Schlesinger warnt vor Inflationspotentiall', *Süddeutsche Zeitung*, 26–27 July 1986. German inflation had fallen to −0.5%, and Schlesinger's speech responded directly to US pressures for fiscal stimulus in Germany. See 'W. German consumer prices declined 0.5% during July', *Wall Street Journal*, 29 July 1986. The Germans continued to resist American pressure throughout the autumn. Finance Minister Gerhard Stoltenberg remarked during a Bundestag debate that the 'artificial stimulation of demand, using fiscal and monetary policies as a lever

for strong international demand' would be counter-productive, and
Chancellor Kohl rejected French demands to stimulate domestic
demand, saying that 'interest rates were the business of the central
bank and the Bundesbank's autonomy had served Germany well'.
'Fear of inflation governs Bonn's thinking', *Wall Street Journal*,
14 September 1986.

26 *Report of the Deutsche Bundesbank for the Year 1987*, p. 8.
27 Ibid., p. 15.
28 Ibid., p. 14.
29 Ibid., p. 17.
30 Ibid., p. 36.
31 Ibid., p. 31.
32 *Report of the Deutsche Bundesbank for the Year 1985*, p. 34.
33 Ibid., p. 38.
34 Helmut Schlesinger, 'Kontinuität in den Zielen, Wandel in den
    Methoden', in Filc et al., p. 197.
35 The increase in August on repurchase agreements was slight, from
    3.55% (July) to 3.60% (August), and there was no public reaction.
    The Bundesbank's interest-rate policy over summer 1987 was intended
    to get the money supply, which was increasing by 7.4% over the 1986
    figure, back into the corridor of 3–6% declared for 1987. This
    objective was reaffirmed by the CBC on 2 July 1987. The Bank's
    review of economic activity in Germany during summer 1987
    emphasized the strong increases in demand, with a real increase in
    GNP of about 1.5% during the first quarter. See *Monthly Report of
    the Deutsche Bundesbank*, vol. 39, no. 9, September 1987, pp. 5–12.
36 'Weltwirtschaftliches Umfeld', Deutsche Bundesbank, *Auszüge aus
    Presseartikeln*, no. 32 (17 April 1989), pp. 2–3.
37 Ibid., p. 2: Britain's deficit is singled out by the Bundesbank.
38 Interest-rate changes were as follows: Discount – from 4% to 4.5%;
    Lombard – from 6% to 6.5%.
39 Claus Köhler, 'Economic Policy in a Framework of Internationalized
    Economic Relations', in Philip Arestis (ed.), *Contemporary Issues in
    Money and Banking: Essays in Honour of Stephen Frowen* (London:
    Macmillan, 1988), p. 87.

Chapter 5

1 Walter Hallstein was the State Secretary of the Federal Germany
   Foreign Ministry and Chief of the German delegation to the
   European Coal and Steel Community (ECSC) – a position which gave
   him the opportunity to shape the realization of the Schumann Plan in
   fundamental ways. With Jean Monnet, Hallstein saw the ECSC as the

beginning of a European community. See Hallstein, *Die Europäische Gemeinschaft* (Düsseldorf: Econ Verlag, 1974).

2 Chaired by Pierre Werner, then Minister-President of Luxembourg, this EC committee set out a vision of Europe as a single area of equal prosperity and substantially greater economic fairness. It incorporated the proposal for a free-trade zone from which national barriers to the movement of goods, services, persons and capital had disappeared without disadvantage to any regions or the creation of new inequalities. The Werner Report also proposed to resolve an increasing number of economic policy issues at the Community level, gradually supplanting the national decision-making institutions of the member states. Unrestricted convertibility of currencies, completely liberal capital movements throughout Europe and fixed exchange rates would be achieved in the last stage of monetary development. For an overview of these developments, see Wolfram E. Hanreider, *Germany, America, Europe: 40 Years of German Foreign Policy* (New Haven: Yale University Press, 1989), pp. 285ff.

3 The European Council approved the EMS in December 1978 and it came into effect on 13 March 1979.

4 Defined in terms of a 'basket' of currencies which includes those of all members of the EMS, viz Germany, France, Benelux, Britain, Ireland, Italy and Denmark.

5 'Judging from past experience, an attempt to defend exchange rates that have ceased to be credible leads to an increase in interventions and thus to a rapid reduction in the monetary autonomy of the countries with more stable currencies.' *Monthly Report of the Deutsche Bundesbank*, no. 3, March 1979.

6 Personal interview with Helmut Schmidt, February 1989. The Bundesbank noted in a letter to the author (29 September 1989) that minutes of the Central Bank Council meeting attended by Schmidt to discuss EMS do not record such a threat. According to Bundesbank sources strict limitations on the European Fund were among the concessions the Bank secured from the German government, a domestic compromise that went against French wishes. See also Schmidt, 'Die Bürokraten ausgetrickst', *Die Zeit*, no. 35, 24 August 1990.

7 'Emminger: kein Schuttabladeplatz für Dollar. Die D-Mark ist keine Reservewährung. Vorerst keine spekulativen Devisenzuflüsse mehr', *Frankfurter Allgemeine Zeitung*, 27 September 1979.

8 Hans-Eckart Scharrer, 'Monetary Policy in Post-War Germany: Between Internal and External Equilibrium', unpublished manuscript, pp. 28–31.

9 Scharrer notes: 'The notion of an "unavoidable" rate is an acknowledgement of the macroeconomic costs and risks involved in too rapid a deceleration of inflation to the medium-term norm, or in sticking to a fixed target of (low) price increases in the face of external shocks.' Ibid., p. 30.

10 At least one German economist argues that the future European central bank should be more independent of government directives than the Bundesbank is now. Such autonomy can only be achieved if governments relinquish their authority over exchange-rate parities to the central banks now. Manfred J.M. Neumann, 'Währungen im Wettbewerb. Die europäischen Notenbanken sollten mit wertbeständigem Geld um die Gunst des Publikums werben. Eine Alternative zum Delors-Plan', *Frankfurter Allgemeine Zeitung*, 5 May 1990.

11 Although theoretically outside the control of the central bank, this increase in the money supply can in practice be 'sterilized' and its effects neutralized in several ways. These are primarily: (1) opposite market operations such as redepositing the weak currency in the market or financing the entire transaction from reserve already held by the central bank in question ('liquidity-neutral financing'); (2) domestic policy that counteracts the foreign currency transactions; (3) short-term financing interventions; (4) through the EMS monthly settlement procedure when it is made in the creditor's currency. Rolf Caesar, 'German Monetary Policy and the European Monetary System', in D.E. Fair and C. de Boissieu (eds.), *International Monetary and Financial Integration – the European Dimension* (Dordrecht: Martinus Nijhoff, 1988), pp. 104–5.

The foreign currency reserves of the Bundesbank place it in a very good position to make such interventions. While these reserves are held with the consent of the other central bank, they reflect factors such as the international demand for the mark and German trade surpluses.

12 The first two entail liquidity effects for the 'weak' and the 'strong' currency, expanding the supply of the latter and contracting the supply of the weak currency as it is removed from the market. For the strong currency there is a resultant increase in its money supply, as money is created to carry out the intervention. Intramarginal interventions produce similar effects if they are executed with funds from either the EMCF or another central bank. Caesar, 'German Monetary Policy', p. 104.

13 In March 1989 Karl Otto Pöhl remarked: 'We can say that, all things considered, the decision for the EMS was the right one. Not all its promises were fulfilled ... But – and this is the decisive thing – it has

been possible to keep prices and exchange rates considerably more stable. Differences in the rate at which money loses its value have become very much smaller; the rates themselves are at their lowest level. Variations in real and nominal exchange rates in the EMS have decreased similarly.' Pöhl, 'Vom Währungssystem zur Währungsunion. Eine politische Entscheidung ist erforderlich, aber keine politische Union', *Auszüge aus Presseartikeln*, no. 22, 10 March 1989.

14 *Report of the Deutsche Bundesbank for the Year 1986*, p. 73.

15 'Im Zeichen von Nyborg', *Frankfurter Allgemeine Zeitung*, 27 August 1987.

16 Bernhard Blohm, 'Zorn auf den Zuchtmeister', *Die Zeit*, 9 October 1987.

17 *Report of the Deutsche Bundesbank for the Year 1987*, p. 68.

18 *Report of the Deutsche Bundesbank for the Year 1986*, pp. 73–4.

19 The French discount rate remained at 9.5% from 1980 to 1988 while the German discount rate varied as follows: 1980: 7.5%; 1981: 7.5%; 1982: 5%; 1983: 4%; 1984: 4.5%; 1985: 4%; 1986: 3.5%; 1987: 2.5%; 1988: 3.5%. IMF, *1989 International Financial Statistics*, pp. 371 and 359.

20 This can be set against Germany's average inflation over the last 40 years of 2.7%, compared to the French figure of 6.7%.

21 Commenting at the end of January 1989 on a rise in German interest rates, Pöhl defended the system's dependence on Germany's monetary stability as 'an anchor of the system that sets the stability standard for other members of the exchange rate federation'. Karl Otto Pöhl, 'Aktuelle Fragen der Währungspolitik', *Auszüge aus Presseartikeln*, no. 9, 27 January 1989, p. 3.

22 Signatories were committed to 'encouraging cooperation between both countries, increasing . . . coordination and harmonizing their economic policies and international financial and economic positions as far as possible'.

23 The draft specified the following purposes: (1) to discuss the outlines of each national economic policy before these were decided by their respective governments and parliaments; (2) to discuss the general economic situation and economic policy of both countries with the goal of their 'maximum possible coordination'; (3) to discuss the international and European economic policies of each country with the goal of their 'maximum possible coordination'; (4) to determine as far as possible the positions to be taken by each country in international negotiations on economic issues.

24 The Bundesbank regarded the Treaty as a serious challenge to its position, with potentially much more far-reaching consequences than

the Plaza and Louvre agreements: 'Kein Hinweis auf Stabilitätsziel', *Frankfurter Allgemeine Zeitung*, 27 January 1988.

25 Treaty provisions seemed designed to fit governmental structures in France but not in Germany. The Bundesbank is independent of the Finance Ministry but the Banque de France is subordinate to the French Finance Minister. The Treaty implied a similar arrangement in noting that Council members would seek 'agreement for all decisions that fall into the area of [the Finance Minister's] responsibility.' Two other aspects of the Treaty worried Bundesbank officials. The institutional responsibilities of the new Council's members were unclear, and its passage on 'harmonization' of economic policy implied Bundesbank subservience to putative policy directives taken in meetings of the Franco-German Council. After ratification by both parliaments, the Treaty would come into full effect in German public law. Through the principle of precedent, it would change the law of the Bundesbank.

26 Simultaneously the government published a position paper clarifying its intentions with respect to the Franco-German Treaty that stressed its 'unambiguously European perspective' and the 'legitimate wishes of the people for harmonization' of French and German economic policy. 'The Deutsche Bundesbank is represented in the Council by its president. I cannot see that the Bundesbank's independence is affected by that. We Germans know through our own painful experience how valuable an independent central bank, dedicated to the goal of price stability, is.' 'Kohl betönt Unabhängigkeit der Bundesbank. Deutsch-französischer Finanz-und Wirtschaftsrat darf den gesetzlichen Auftrag der Notenbank nicht gefährden', *Börsen-Zeitung*, 5 February 1988.

27 The Bundesbank was given highly visible support by the Organization for the Protection of German Savers (*Gemeinschaft zum Schutz der deutschen Sparer*) – a politically significant group in a country accustomed to investing its savings in conservative vehicles, primarily deposit accounts. 'Bundesbank soll Unabhängigkeit nützen. Sparerschützer mahnen – Stellungnahme zum deutsch-fransözischen Finanz und Wirtschaftsrat', *Börsen-Zeitung*, 6 April 1988. 'Offener Streit zwischen Bonn und Bundesbank', *Süddeutsche Zeitung*, 22 January 1988.

28 The first such visit in over twenty years. Accounts of the session report it as a 'private lesson in monetary stability' – and hence in the Bundesbank's prerogatives – for Kohl. 'Ein Privatissme für Kohl zur Währungsautonomie', *Handelsblatt*, 15 June 1988.

29 A declaration following the 16 September meeting included an announcement that both sides could live with the present franc-mark rate and a pledge to work for price stability by both sides. 'Paris und

Bonn betonen Wähungsstabilität', *Süddeutsche Zeitung*, 17 September 1988; 'Guter Wille über Alles', *Die Zeit*, 16 September 1988.

30 See Hans-Dietrich Genscher, 'Die Rolle der Bundesrepublik Deutschland bei der Vollendung der Europäischen Währungsunion', in Bertelsmann Stiftung, *Die Vollendung des EWS: Ergebnisse einer Fachtagung* (Gütersloh: Bertelsmann, 1989). Genscher here conforms to the 'German consensus' that a European Central Bank must be dedicated to stability, politically independent, federal and prohibited from financing government deficits (pp. 18–19).

31 *The Financial Times*, 27 June 1988.

32 Ibid.

33 Its members included the heads of European central banks, the General Manager of the Bank for International Settlements in Basle, the President of the Banco Exterior de Espana, and Niels Tygesen (Professor of Economics, Copenhagen).

34 Published on 20 April 1989 (doc. no. 1550/1551).

35 France and Germany are each other's largest European trading partners. Germany runs a consistent trade surplus with France, a situation that prompts frequent calls for 'recycling' of these surpluses.

36 See Peter-W. Schlüter, 'Währungspolitik', in Werner Weidenfeld and Wolfgang Wessels (eds.), *Jahrbuch der Europäischen Integration 1986/87* (Bonn: Europa Verlag, 1987), pp. 128–40.

37 Commenting in 1985 on liberalization of its capital markets, the Bundesbank reported that unmanageable capital imports had not occurred despite the large German current account surplus (36 billion marks, or 0.7% of GNP). Dollar investments had become more attractive as US growth increased and 'the inflows of funds which had formerly narrowed the Bundesbank's room for manoeuvre considerably were lacking'. Moreover, 'the speculative movements of funds which had been recorded before and after realignments of the exchange rates in the [EMS] were of orders of magnitude which ... did not prove dangerous to monetary policy'. *Monthly Report of the Deutsche Bundesbank*, vol. 37, no. 7, July 1985, p. 19.

38 Rolf Caesar comments that 'only in 1982 and 1983 does the EMS seem to have globally dominated the Bundesbank's NEP (net external position) and, thereby, the creation of base money via the "external component". Moreover it should be stressed that the net liquidity effects of the EMS were nearly zero in 1984/1985.' Caesar, 'German Monetary Policy', p. 106. Money supply targets were met in every year except 1980/81 during the period from 1979 to 1985. The overshooting that occurred in 1986–9 cannot be accounted for in terms of the Bundesbank's EMS obligations.

39 The Bank tends to understate the effects of unexpected events on its money supply targets, but conceded that 1983 and 1986 caused

monetary disturbances which could not be controlled after the
first round of intervention. Caesar, 'German Monetary Policy',
pp. 111–12. See also *Report of the Deutsche Bundesbank for the Year
1983*, p. 24, and *Monthly Report of the Deutsche Bundesbank*, June
1986, p. 12.

40 See the argument by Rolf Caesar, in 'German Monetary Policy',
pp. 114–22, that while the EMS has not seriously affected the money
supply, that 'does not mean the EMS has not been responsible for any
imported inflation. Rather, every system of stable exchange rates
tends to establish an international connection of inflation via
international price relationships.'

41 An 'economist' theory defines money as a representative good whose
value is tied to the economic fundamentals of a particular system.
Thus domestic inflation and exchange rates, both monetary relations,
are necessarily linked to economic factors such as productivity and
investment as well as fiscal policy. There must be substantial
convergence of domestic national economies or monetary integration
will fail, ending as an 'inflationary community'. 'Monetarist' theory
reverses those relationships, looking to money as a transformative
factor for the economy in general and exchange rates as instruments
for achieving national economic integration and political unity in
Europe. Institutional reforms including a European central bank and
establishment of the ecu as a parallel currency have been the
monetarists' main goals, and these have been promoted as means to
lessen continuing divergence in economic fundamentals. Heidemarie
C. Sherman, 'Central Banking in Germany and the Process of
European Monetary Integration', *Tokyo Club Papers*, No. 3, 1990
(Tokyo: Tokyo Club Foundation for Global Studies, 1989), p. 169.
See also Norbert Kloten, 'Das Europäische Währungssystem – eine
europäische Grundentscheidung im Rückblick', *Rheinisch-Westfälische
Akademie der Wissenschaften* (Oplanden: Westdeutscher Verlag, 1980).

42 Norbert Kloten, 'Aspekte eines europäischen Zentralbanksystems',
WISU-Magazin, November 1988. For an excellent analysis of
European currency proposals as requiring 'fundamental constitutional
decisions', see Kloten, 'Das Europäische Währungssystem'.

In recent years sovereignty has been an almost exclusively British
concern. Reversing their position under de Gaulle, the French now
vigorously press for a formal transfer of national authority to
European institutions. Whether such supranational political
organizations as the European Parliament or the technocratic agencies
of the European Commission will ever enjoy the basic loyalties which
citizens of the various European countries now feel towards their
countries is fundamental for the stability of any future European

federation. Mrs Thatcher's awareness of the power of populist sentiments for traditional political organizations and against 'Brussels bureaucrats' accounted in part at least for her arguments against monetary union. Even more moderate opponents of a single currency and a European central bank argue that such a transformation could take place through democratically legitimated processes – a European parliament perceived as more representative of popular will than of particular national interests.

43 Wilhelm Nölling, *Fortress Europe? The External Trade Policy of the European Community. Response to the Challenge of 1992* (Hamburger Beiträge zur Wirtschafts- und Währungspolitik in Europa, 1988).

44 Kloten, 'Das Europäische Währungssystem'.

Chapter 6

1 During discussions between the federal government and the Bundesbank leading up to German Economic and Monetary Union, the Bank warned 'Should wages be exchanged [from Ostmark to Deutschmark value] on a 1:1 basis and should an unrealistic price structure only be corrected after the conversion, then the necessarily large price increases for so-called basic needs would create the danger of a price-wage spiral – a danger that the Bundesbank must call attention to in advance because of its primary responsibility for the stability of the D-mark, and which it is essential to prevent.' Deutsche Bundesbank, *Pressenotiz*, 2 April 1990, p. 3.

2 Although it is not clear how great the strain will be. Estimates on the cost of rebuilding productive capacity in East Germany range from DM 259 billion to DM 1,200 billion. Additional indirect costs of unification, such as unemployment benefit, pensions and other social services would also be incurred and might run to DM 25 billion. The Bundesbank's internal estimates of the fundamentals of East Germany's economy before July 1990 varied so widely that some officials regarded them as highly speculative. There were no reliable figures, for example, on the velocity of money, a key variable in the Bundesbank calculus of inflation.

3 A survey by the Allensbach Institute in September 1988 found the Bundesbank ranked third among federal German institutions, after the President and the Constitutional Court. Of those interviewed, 50% had a positive opinion of it, and only 3% a negative one.

4 If a compromise is the result, the Bundesbank appears to be relying on a British veto, not its own government. Interview with Karl Otto Pöhl by Hugo Young, 'The Demon Banker', *Guardian*, 7 September 1990.

5 *Report of the Deutsche Bundesbank for the Year 1989*, p. 9.

6 Ibid., pp. 9–13.
7 Shortly after German unification, Hans Tietmeyer warned government leaders, especially Helmut Kohl, that unrestrained borrowing on the capital markets was unacceptable to the Bundesbank. It does not intend to go along with bond issues to cover the public sector borrowing requirement for the next two years, and the Bank commented – in tones that echoed its conflict with Helmut Schmidt in 1980–81 – that cuts in public spending were necessary to make capital available to the eastern Länder. See 'Bundesbank opposes debt to fund unity. German central bank says the policy may force it to raise its interest rates', *Wall Street Journal*, 24 October 1990.

BIBLIOGRAPHY

This bibliography lists useful books and articles not already cited in the Notes.

Books

Buiter, W.H., and Marston, R.C. (eds.), *International Economic Policy Coordination*. Cambridge: Cambridge University Press, 1985.

Burgess, M., *Federalism and European Union: Political Ideas, Influences and Strategies in the European Community, 1972–1986*. London: Routledge & Kegan Paul, 1989.

Crockett, A., and Goldstein, M., *Strengthening the International Monetary System: Exchange Rates, Surveillance, and Objective Indicators*. Washington, DC: International Monetary Fund, 1987.

Emerson, M., et al., *The Economics of 1992: The EC Commission's Assessment of the Economic Effects of Completing the Internal Market*. Oxford: Oxford University Press, 1988.

Giavazzi, F., Micossi, S., and Miller, M. (eds.), *The European Monetary System*. Cambridge: Cambridge University Press, 1988.

Gleske, Leonard, *Probleme und Perspektiven der internationalen Währungsentwicklung*. Tübingen: J.C.B. Mohr (Paul Siebeck), 1988.

Guerrieri, P., and Padoan, P.C. (eds.), *The Political Economy of European Integration*. New York: Harvester Wheatsheaf, 1989.

Hibbs, Douglas, *The Political Economy of Industrial Democracies*. Cambridge, MA: Harvard University Press, 1988.

Issing, Otmar (ed.), *Wechselkursstabilisierung, EWS und Weltwährungssystem*. Hamburg: 1988.

Keohane, R.O., *After Hegemony*. Princeton: Princeton University Press, 1984.

Kommers, Donald P., *The Constitutional Jurisprudence of the Federal Republic of Germany*. Durham, NC: Duke University Press, 1988.

Lindberg, L.N., and Maier, C.S., *The Politics of Inflation and Economic Stagnation*. Washington, DC: The Brookings Institution, 1985.

Milward, A.S., *The Reconstruction of Western Europe 1945-51*. Berkeley UP: California, 1984.

Odell, J., *US International Monetary Policy: Markets, Power, Ideas as Sources of Change*. Princeton, 1982.

Padoa-Schioppa, T., *Lessons from the EMS*. Florence: European University Institute, 1986.

Schmidt, H., *Menschen und Mächte*. Berlin: Siedler Verlag, 1987.

Schonfield, A., *Modern Capitalism*. Oxford: Oxford University Press, 1985.

Simonian, H., *The Privileged Partnership: Franco-German Relations in the European Community, 1969-84*. New York: Oxford University Press, 1985.

Taylor, P., *The Limits of European Integration*. London: Croom Helm, 1983.

Wallace, H., Wallace, W., and Webb, C. (eds.), *Policy-Making in the European Community*. New York: John Wiley, 1983.

Wessels, W., and Regelsberger, E. (eds.), *The Federal Republic of Germany and the European Community: The Presidency and Beyond*. Bonn: Europa Union, 1988.

Articles

Note: The following abbreviations have been used:

AP   Deutsche Bundesbank, *Auszüge aus Presseartikeln*
BZ   *Börsen-Zeitung*
FAZ   *Frankfurter Allgemeine Zeitung*

Almond, G., 'Review article: The international-national connection', *British Journal of Political Science* (19) 1989, 237-59.

Baehring, B., 'Kein Feldherrnhügel der Deutschen Bundesbank', *BZ*, 4 May 1988.

Baehring, B., 'Die Bundesbank Präsidenten': (1) 'Macht und Gefährdung

des Amtes', *BZ*, 3 August 1982; (2) 'Die Zeiten ändern sich', *BZ*,
4 August 1982; (3) 'Die Zeiten haben sich geändert', *BZ*, 4 August
1982; (4) 'Experte auf dem Prüfstand', *BZ*, 6 August 1982.

Barbier, H.D., 'Die Bundesbank in den Zwängen der Außenpolitik.
Bundesbank Präsident Pöhl über Chancen und Risiken der
koordinierten Wirtschaftspolitik', *FAZ*, 20 September 1988.

Caesar, R., 'Bundesbank-Autonomie: Internationale Bedrohungen?',
Wirtschaftsdienst, March 1988.

Camdessus, Michel, 'Die währungspolitische Zusammenarbeit aus
französischer Sicht', *Sparkasse*, January 1987.

Dresdner Bank, 'Acht Jahre EWS: Erfolge und Probleme', *Dresdner Bank
Wirtschaftsberichte*, July 1987.

Fels, Joachim, 'The EMS 1979–1987: why has it worked?', *Intereconomics*
no. 5, 1987.

Fleming, S., 'Schmidt hits at Bundesbank's monetary policy', *The
Financial Times*, 14 April 1981.

Genscher, Hans-Dietrich, 'Memorandum für die Schaffung eines
europäischen Währungsraumes und einer europäischen Zentralbank',
AP, no. 15, 1 March 1988.

Giavazzi, F., and Giovannini, A., 'Models of the EMS: is Europe a
greater Deutschemark area?', in R. C. Bryant, and R. Portes (eds.),
Global Macroeconomics: Policy Conflict and Cooperation. London:
Macmillan, 1988.

Gleske, L., 'Exchange rates, interventions and monetary policy – a central
banker's view', *AP*, no. 20, 17 March 1987.

Gleske, L., 'The Deutsche Bundesbank as partner in monetary policy
cooperation', *American Banker*, 10 June 1988.

Gleske, L., 'Devisenmarktinterventionen der Deutschen Bundesbank', in
Engels, *Internationaler Kapitalverkehr und Devisenhandel*. Frankfurt:
F. Knapp, 1986.

Gleske, L., 'Die Geldmarktpolitik der Bundesbank. Erfahrungen und
Probleme', in W. Filc, et al., *Herausforderungen der Wirtschaftspolitik*.
Berlin: Duncker and Humblot, 1988.

Hoffman, Stanley, 'The European Community and 1992', *Foreign Affairs*,
vol. 68, Winter 1989–90.

Issing, O., 'Europäische Notenbank – ein Phantom', *FAZ*, 12 March
1988.

Issing, O., 'Die Unabhängigkeit der Bundesbank, theoretisch umstritten,
praktisch bewährt', in W. Ehrlicher and D. Simmert, *Geld- und
Währungspolitik in der Bundesrepublik Deutschland*. Berlin: Duncker
and Humblot, 1982.

Johnson, K., and Painter, C., 'British governments and the EMS', *The
Political Quarterly*, 1980.

Kloten, Norbert, 'Moving towards a European Central Bank System',
AP, no. 46, 23 June 1988.

Kloten, N., 'Paradigmawechsel in der Geldpolitik. Johann-Heinrich von
Thünnen-Vorlesung am 14.9.1987', *AP*, no. 67, 18 September 1987.

Kloten, N., 'Tracks towards a common monetary policy in Europe', *AP*,
no. 65, 1987.

Köhler, Claus, 'Probleme der monetären Strategie in der Bundesrepublik
Deutschland', in W. Ehrlicher and W. Simmert, *Geld- und
Währungspolitik*.

Köhler, Claus, 'National monetary policy in an open world economy',
AP, no. 26, 9 April 1987.

Loehnis, Anthony, 'A British View of a European Central Bank. Speech
to the "European Currency" Group of the European Parliament,
Strasbourg, 15.6.1988'. Bank for International Settlements, *Business
Review* no. 144, 25 July 1988.

Nölling, Wilhelm, 'Eine Mark muß immer eine Mark bleiben', *Die Welt*,
13–14 February 1988.

Pöhl, Karl Otto, 'Die Vision eines europäischen Währungsraumes. Was
zu tun wäre', *FAZ*, 28 May 1988.

Pöhl, K. O., 'Widersprüche und Gemeinsamkeiten in der Politik der
Bundesregierung und der Deutschen Bundesbank in der Zeit von
1978–1982', in H. Schmidt and W. Hesselbach (eds.), *Kämpfer ohne
Pathos. Festschrift für Hans Matthöfer zum 60. Geburtstag am
25. September 1985*. Bonn: Verlag Neue Gesellschaft, 1985.

Pöhl, K. O., 'Cooperation – a keystone for the stability of the
international monetary system', first Arthur Burns memorial lecture at
the American Council on Germany, New York, 2 November 1987,
AP, no. 79, 3 November 1987.

Pöhl, K. O., 'The EMS – a model for a more stable international
monetary order', *AP*, no. 33, 6 May 1987.

Pöhl, K. O., 'The globalization of financial markets and its impact on the
international monetary system', *AP*, no. 29, 25 April 1988.

Pöhl, K. O., 'Die Politik der Bundesbank im Spannungsfeld der
nationalen und internationalen Währungspolitik. Vortrag anlässlich
des 20. List-Gesprächs in Frankfurt/M. am 5 April 1984', *AP*, no. 30,
12 April 1984.

Pöhl, K. O., 'Vierzig Jahre D-Mark. Ansprache beim Festakt zum 40.
Jahrestag der Währungsreform', *AP*, no. 43, 15 June 1988.

Pöhl, K. O., 'Vom Währungssystem zur Währungsunion. Eine politische
Entscheidung ist erforderlich, aber keine politische Union', *AP*,
no. 22, 10 March 1989.

Putnam, R.D., and Henning, C. R., 'The Bonn summit of 1978: how does
international economic policy coordination really work?', in R. N.

Cooper, B. Eichengreen, and G. Holtham (eds.), *Can Nations Agree? Issues in International Economic Cooperation*, Washington, DC: The Brookings Institution, 1989.

Sandholtz, W., and Zysman, J., '1992: Recasting the European Bargain', *World Politics*, vol. 42, October 1989.

Scharrer, Hans-Eckart, 'A European Central Bank?', *Intereconomics*, March-April 1988.

Scharrer, H.-E., 'Currencies and Hedging in German Foreign Trade', in *Studies on Economic and Monetary Problems and on Banking History*. Frankfurt: Deutsche Bank, 1980.

Schlesinger, Helmut, 'Das Konzept der Deutschen Bundesbank', in W. Ehrlicher and W. Simmert, *Wandlungen des geldpolitischen Instrumentariums der Deutschen Bundesbank*. Berlin: Duncker and Humblot, 1988.

Schlesinger, H., 'Politik für einen stabilen Geldwert', *AP*, no. 37, 25 May 1988.

Schlüter, Peter-Wilhelm, 'Die Stellung des EWS im Weltwährungssystem', in O. Issing (ed.), *Wechselkursstabilisierung, EWS und Weltwährungssystem*. Hamburg: 1988.

Schmidt, Helmut, 'Währungspolitik in Europa blockiert von Kleinmütigen', *Die Zeit*, 22 April 1988.

Seuss, W., 'Der Zorn des Kanzlers. Zum Konflikt mit der Bundesbank', *FAZ*, 15 April 1981.

Tietmeyer, Hans, 'Aktuelle Fragen der europäischen und internationalen Währungspolitik', *Zeitschrift für Wirtschaftspolitik*, 1986.

Werner, Pierre, 'Die nächste Stufe zur Währungsunion', *BZ*, 23 June 1988.

Williamson, J, 'The failure of world monetary reform: a reassessment', in Cooper et al., *The International Monetary System under Flexible Exchange Rates*. Cambridge, MA: Ballinger, 1982.

Wood, Geoffrey, 'European Monetary Integration? A Review Essay', *Journal of Monetary Economics*, 1986.

CHATHAM HOUSE PAPERS
Also in this series

Financing the European Community
Michael Shackleton
This study examines the implications of important innovations made by the February 1988 Delors package and subsequent institutional decisions for the future financing of the EC. Published March 1990

The New Eastern Europe:
Western Resposes
J.M.C. Rollo
'... readable, up-to-date, relevant and concise ... once again Chatham House's team of experts has produced the right briefing at the right time.' - George Robertson, *The House Magazine* (weekly journal of the Houses of Parliament) Published April 1990

Global Companies and Public Policy:
The Growing Challenge of FDI
DeAnne Julius
'... will help everyone who wants to understand how the world economy is changing and the implications for national politics ... calls into question some of the fundamental assumptions on which trade and exchange-rate policies are based.' - Peter B. Kenen, Princeton University. Published April 1990

European Competition Policy
edited by Peter Montagnon
'... a very timely look at an area of Community politics that is at the heart of the 1992 programme ... Peter Montagnon tackles the subject with precision and authority, and achieves the difficult task of writing a book that makes sense to the layman while retaining credibility with the specialist.' - Giles Merritt, *The Financial Times*
Published September 1990

Britain's Future in Europe
Michael Franklin with Marc Wilke
This highly topical book examines the main policy areas currently preoccupying the European Community, and seeks to determine how Britain can best play a useful role in shaping the Community's development. Published December 1990

RIIA/PINTER PUBLISHERS